LISA PELIO-HYDE

SHATTERED-
BUT
GOD

A Body Utterly Shattered And The
Complete Healing And Restoration By
The Miraculous Hand Of God

First Edition © 2018

Copyright © 2018 by Lisa Pelio-Hyde

www.pelioarts.com

All rights reserved. No part of this book may be used or reproduced by any means, graphic, electronic, or mechanical, including photocopying, recording, taping or by any information storage retrieval system without the written permission of Lisa Pelio-Hyde except in the case of brief quotations embodied in critical articles and reviews.

Rejoice Essential Publishing

PO BOX 512

Effingham, SC 29541

www.republishing.org

Back cover photo of Lisa taken by Jennie Boyce-Bold Tree Photography

Unless otherwise indicated, Scripture is taken from the King James Version.

Scripture quotations marked (NKJV) are taken from the New King James Version®. Copyright ©1982 by Thomas Nelson. Used by permission. All rights reserved.

Scripture quotations marked (NIV) are taken from the Holy Bible, New International Version®,

NIV®. Copyright ©1973, 1978, 1984, 2011 by Biblica, Inc.™ Used by permission of Zondervan. All rights reserved.

Shattered-But God/ Lisa Pelio-Hyde

ISBN-10:1-946756-44-X

ISBN-13:978-1-946756-44-2

Library of Congress Control Number: 2018964338

DEDICATION

This book is dedicated lovingly to my precious husband and son, whose unending courage, loyalty, and devotion continue to strengthen me.

Shattered-But God is a must read for anyone going through any trials or tribulations concerning your health. Lisa goes into great detail about her health experience and how God miraculously healed and restored her. This book will definitely encourage you in the faith and remind you that God is faithful no matter what circumstances you may be going through. God is still in the healing business and performing miracles every day!

Bishop Ron Webb

TABLE OF CONTENTS

INTRODUCTION.................................1

CHAPTER 1:   A DAY LIKE NO OTHER.....................2

CHAPTER 2:   FINALLY THE HOSPITAL 5

CHAPTER 3:   THE POWER OF GOD......................16

CHAPTER 4:   TWO REALITIES........21

CHAPTER 5:   GOD WAS ALWAYS WITH ME 25

CHAPTER 6:   THE LORD IS MY STRENGTH...............32

CHAPTER 7:   GOD HAD US IN JUST THE RIGHT PLACE......................38

CHAPTER 8:   TIME IS SHORT........41

CHAPTER 9:   TAKING THE NEXT BIG STEP..................44

CHAPTER 10:	CAN I GO HOME YET?..........................53
CHAPTER 11:	DISCERNING THE SIGNS OF OUR TIMES........58
CHAPTER 12:	HOME FOR CHRISTMAS..............64
CHAPTER 13:	THE MERRIEST OF CHRISTMASES........72
CHAPTER 14:	WE GOT THIS............76
CHAPTER 15:	LITTLE THINGS MEAN A LOT.........................80
CHAPTER 16:	ALMOST THERE.......83
CHAPTER 17:	LIGHT AT THE END OF THE TUNNEL......93
CHAPTER 18:	PRAISE GOD FOR TOTAL RESTORATION.......101
CHAPTER 19:	HOME FROM A LONG JOURNEY....109

CHAPTER 20: TWO TRUTHS - A MIRACLE AND THE GUT 119

CHAPTER 21: THE EASTER MIRACLE 137

CONCLUSION: 144

ABOUT THE AUTHOR 146

REFERENCES 149

GLOSSARY 151

INTRODUCTION

The story I'm about to convey to you is a true story. It is a story that happened to me. A story that I lived. The story of a body that was Shattered-But God. Even though my body was utterly shattered, it was never wholly destroyed and how it was touched and ultimately healed and restored by the miraculous hand of Almighty God. This is my testimony to my Lord and Savior Jesus Christ. A testimony that Jesus Christ is alive! He is risen and is seated at the right hand of the Father and from there, each and every day, He performs mighty miracles. No event occurs by coincidence, but happens by reason and serves a purpose. This must be unequivocally understood for what I'm about to relay to you. I am in the midst of a miracle that continues to this day. I'm a living, breathing, walking, talking, miracle of God. The hand of God intervened in my life mightily. I marvel at the miracle that I have experienced, and I desire to share my story with you.

CHAPTER 1

A DAY LIKE NO OTHER

I'll never forget that day. Memories of that morning and what was to come are still vivid. It would be a day like no other. We had settled into our lovely new home with a very comfortable life in Missouri. We had acquired many new friendships and were settling into our new routine. It was an absolutely beautiful autumn day in the Ozarks. The leaves were a vibrant blend of red-orange and gold upon the trees, and the sky was bright blue and clear. I looked out of the living room window into the valley below and thought to myself, "What an absolutely lovely day." We were eagerly anticipating family coming from Michigan for Thanksgiving, and I was busily decorating the house in all of its autumn splendor. My husband had taken our son to school as usual, and I was going about my daily routine of making coffee and getting ready to watch Fox news.

All of a sudden it was as if someone took a filet knife and sliced my intestines. It was the most excruciating pain I had ever experienced in my life. It absolutely took my breath away. I fell back to the coach. I tried to get up and go to the bathroom, but my feet could hardly move. I tried again, this time I managed to rise to my feet. I staggered my way across the room, finally making it to the bathroom.

I heard my husband return, I managed to come out and leaned against the breakfast bar. He looked at me and asked, "What's wrong?" I said, "Something horrible is happening I don't know what it is." He then said, "Well what is it?" I cried out, "Just horrible pain!" "Do you need to go to the hospital?" he hesitantly questioned. I answered with disbelief, "I ... I don't know... yes, I think I do." The look on his face said it all. For I was not one to just go to the hospital unless something was horrifically wrong.

We called 911 and waited for the paramedics to arrive. I began throwing up, and the color of the vomit was black. I knew that wasn't good. When the ambulance finally arrived, we told them we wanted to go to Cox South in Springfield. The paramedics lifted me onto the stretcher, carried me out of the house, and into the ambulance. I couldn't tolerate the pain it was so severe and intense, as if a knife was cutting into my lower abdomen. I couldn't even lay down on the stretcher for the long journey ahead of me to the hospital.

The paramedics that day were so kind and genuinely caring and compassionate. They tried to soothe my every fear and encouraged me as we headed to the hospital. "It's alright. We're taking care of you" they said. "I can't lie down" I cried out to them! "It's okay. Whatever makes you comfortable we will do to get you to the hospital. Just relax," they answered calmly. One medic proceeded to call ahead to Cox to confirm it was okay to give me something to relax so I could tolerate the hour drive to the hospital. It must've worked. For the next thing, I remembered was turning off the highway and in just minutes arriving at the emergency entrance at the hospital. Thank God we had finally arrived!

CHAPTER 2

FINALLY THE HOSPITAL

Upon my arrival at the hospital, all I remember is my dear friend Sally was already there, as well as my husband Jim who followed the ambulance. I remember being in the emergency room and the doctor coming in and saying to me, "Now you are not going to remember much of anything. It might be a day, or it might even be several days, but you will be completely out. But these people will know everything that's going on, and it will be a very long period of time for them." With all that being said, I was calm and had no fear. It was as if I had a wave of peace come over me that could only come from God. And that was the last thing I remembered. Little did I know at the time it would be the last thing I would remember for days going into weeks.

The next thing that happened is absolutely unbelievable. I have no recollection, but everything that I went through and all that transpired over the next several days was retold to me by my husband. I had never heard of anyone having their abdominal cavity open and left open for several days, but that's precisely what happened to me.

The medical staff started a series of antibiotics that continued through the night, but the surgeon said, "We have to act, and we have to act now." I then went in for surgery. He opened my abdomen and found I had a gastrointestinal perforation, or in other words, I had a hole in my large intestine. My entire body had filled with sepsis, and my appendix was engorged. I later found out the appendix hangs from the lower right side of the large intestine. You talk about another miracle; that was it! Having a hole in my large intestine that my appendix was hanging from made it a ticking time bomb, for it was already being affected. Needless to say, he removed my appendix and took out 6 inches of my large intestine. He then began the delicate process of thoroughly washing and cleansing my entire abdominal cavity. This is absolutely necessary for when your G.I. tract is perforated, the contents spill into your abdomen and can cause peritonitis, an infection, and such an infection can and did lead to sepsis. Sometimes this condition is misdiagnosed and incorrectly called blood poisoning.

(Lisa intubated in the Intensive Care Unit 5)[1]

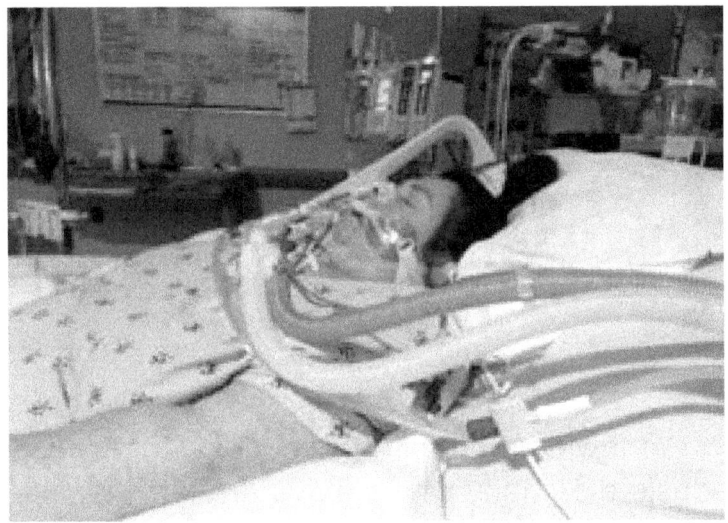

(Urine Catheter)[2]

Worldwide, one-third of people who develop sepsis die. Many who survive are left with life-changing effects such as chronic pain and fatigue, organ dysfunction, and some even suffer from amputations. Sepsis kills and disables millions and requires early diagnosis and treatment for survival. It was only by the hand of God that I received that early diagnosis and immediate treatment for my survival. During that same period of time, I had another procedure which would leave me with a temporary colostomy.

(Sepsis)[3]

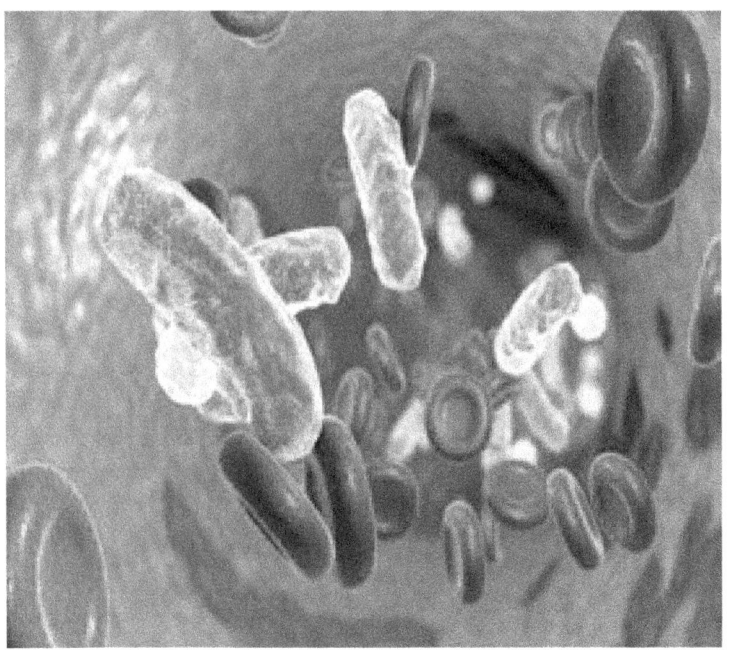

(Sepsis bacteria in blood)[4]

(Colostomy—stoma & Bag ONLY)[5]

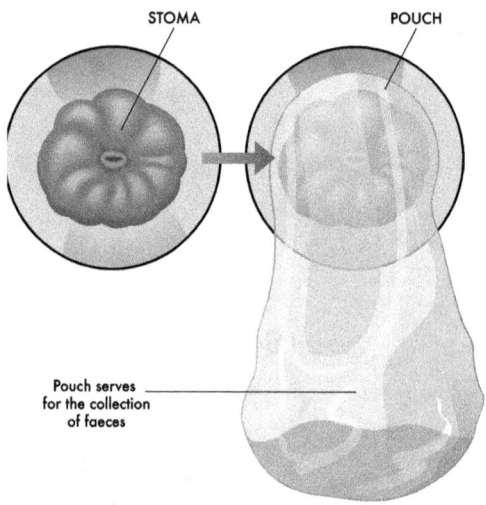

(Stoma Site on Left Image and Colostomy Bag on Right)[6]

The colostomy bag

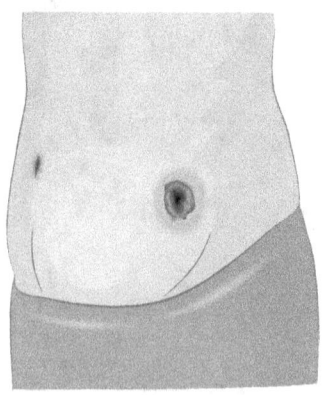
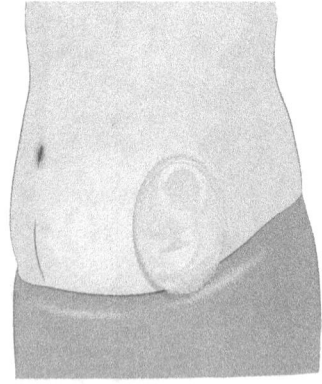

A colostomy is where a stoma or a hole is created in your abdomen, and a colostomy bag is put in place so the contents of your intestine or waste can empty into the bag. Down the road, I would then need another surgery to reverse this procedure and reattach my intestine to my colon. I was also intubated at that time.

The process of washing and cleansing each and every part of my intestine and entire cavity continued meticulously for the next 5 days. It's interesting it was for 5 days. For the number 5 represents 'grace' and God really showed me His grace during that time. The surgeon went back day after day to make sure there was not even a speck of sepsis left in my body. Finally, he was satisfied that all the sepsis and infection was gone. He closed my body, and I remained intubated for the next 4 days while easing me off little by little, bringing me out of my induced state, and finally being completely awake and off the ventilator. This was the beginning of a very long journey, but one that would be victorious through Christ Jesus.

Did you know that there are over 40 different miracles documented in the Bible that are attributed to our Lord Jesus? The very first miracle attributed to Jesus was at a wedding in Canaan where He transformed water into wine John 2:1-11. This was the beginning of many miracles during the earthly ministry of Jesus. These miracles are represented in different categories. The majority are miracles of physical healings, but there were other miracles as well:

- Deliverance through exorcisms, as found in Mark 1:21-28.
- Miracles over His control of nature found in Matthew 8:23-27, Mark 4:35-41, Luke 8:26-33.
- Raising people up from the dead Luke 7:11-17.

The disciple John declares Jesus did more miracles than what has been written about him. We find this in John 21:24-25 (NKJV):

"This is the disciple who testifies of these things, and wrote these things, and we know that his testimony is true. And there are also many other things that Jesus did, which if they were written one by one, I suppose that even the world itself could not contain the books that would be written. Amen."

There are many accounts of Jesus doing miraculous healings in all four Gospels. Here we see but a few:

- Healing the woman with the issue of blood —Matthew 9:20-22, Mark 5:25-34, Luke 8:43-48.
- Healing a man that had been crippled for over 38 years —John 5:1-17.
- Healing a paralyzed man — Matthew 9:2-7, Mark 2:3-12, Luke 5:18-26.
- Healing a man of leprosy — Matthew 8:1-4
- Healing a man with palsy — Luke 5:-17-25
- And of course the ultimate Healing of bringing Lazarus back to life from the dead— John 11:1-44

The last documented miracle in the earthly ministry of Jesus Christ was in the garden of Gethsemane. All the Gospels describe the arrest of Jesus before His crucifixion. All of them relay the tense moments of the arrest and that a follower of Jesus drew a sword and severed the ear of the man named Malchus. In John 18:10 we find out that follower was Peter. In Luke 22:51 we see the details that no other writer gives. Luke tells us that Jesus 'touched the man's ear and healed him.' Here we see even at the final hour of His earthly ministry that Jesus is selfless and cares with such compassion for all of humanity.

As you can see, there are numerous miracles and many more to add to these. If you notice some of these miracles have more than one account. This is significant to show the accuracy of the event. Some of them are documented in all four Gospels which again indicates the validity of each and every miracle. In some miracles, Jesus didn't even have to act His mere presence was enough for people to be healed and made whole. This is where 'faith' comes in. We have to believe and have faith knowing that Jesus will intervene and heal us as He did in the numerous miracles He implemented while He walked the earth. This is evident in the account of the Roman centurion, a Gentile, asking Jesus for help when his servant was ill.

> We find this in Matthew: "When Jesus had entered Capernaum, a centurion came to Him, asking for help. "Lord, He said my servant lies at home paralyzed, suffering terribly." Jesus said to him, "Shall I come and heal him?" The centurion replied, "Lord, I do not deserve to have you come under my roof. But just say the word, and my servant will be healed. For I myself am a man under authority, with soldiers under me. I tell this one, 'Go' and he goes; and that one, 'Come' and he comes. I say to my servant, 'Do this,' and he does it". "When Jesus heard this, He was amazed and said to those who followed, "Truly I tell you, I have not found anyone in Israel with such great faith. I say to

you that many will come from east and west, and will take their places at the feast with Abraham, Isaac and Jacob in the kingdom of heaven. But the subjects of the kingdom will be thrown outside, into the darkness, where there will be weeping and gnashing of teeth." Then Jesus said to the centurion, "Go! Let it be done just as you believed it would." And his servant was healed at that moment. — Matthew 8:5-13 (NIV).

Jesus offered to go to the centurion's house to perform the healing, but the centurion answered by saying, Jesus by Your word of 'authority' from where You are at this moment is sufficient. Jesus commented approvingly on the strong 'faith' displayed by the soldier and that He had not found such great faith not even in Israel and guaranteed the request and the servant was healed that same day. This account is found in the Gospels of Matthew and Luke. This is the 'faith' that we must operate in. We take the 'authority' that has been entrusted to us by Christ Jesus and 'stand' and 'believe' with 'faith' in our miracle and healing today. He gives us the 'authority' right where He is now, seated at the right hand of the Father and all we must do is act.

CHAPTER 3

THE POWER OF GOD

Just recently someone relayed to me that my husband Jim stood by my bedside like a soldier standing guard. He remained unmovable and steadfast in those first crucial days of me being in the hospital. He put out the word and a call for prayer to many of our friends and family during those early critical hours. They responded by lifting me up in prayer and putting my name on multiple prayer lists of several ministries. My husband personally put in a call to a dynamic pastor who graciously arose to the occasion. That pastor was Bishop Ron Webb. Later I would see the texts between the two of them that went out and the urgency from my husband to have him come.

As with all pastors, I know that they are extremely busy, and Bishop Webb is no exception. We had just met him a few months before. The meeting was about another book I had written, and the Lord was very clear about meeting with Bishop Webb in seeking a publisher. I can remember at the time that the Lord was very clear about contacting Bishop Webb and him alone. I thought, "Lord he doesn't even know me. Why would he even call me back if he doesn't know who I am?" The Lord was quite adamant about me contacting Bishop Webb, so I did. Bishop was very gracious and was more than happy to help me. This indeed was a divine appointment or God appointment as I call them. Our meetings were prematurely cut short for my body was then shattered, and this whole journey had begun.

It was in the third month of my journey being home and rebounding from my extended hospital stay, that we went into Springfield on one particular afternoon. We had picked our son up from school and went to Springfield got a bite to eat, and then did some shopping. It was unusual that we were there on a Monday for; usually, we go to Springfield closer to the weekend. However, it was Monday, and that is the night that Bishop Webb has church in Springfield. While there I felt very impressed that we should attend Monday night service at the sister church of Bishop Webb. I told my husband Jim, I felt we needed to go to church that night, and he answered, "Let's go." So we went.

The presence of the Holy Spirit was so strong that night and continued from the beginning of worship to the end of the service with a call for all needing a touch from the Lord. Bishop Webb looked out into the congregation and saw me, my husband, and our son. He called me up and asked if I would give my testimony. I went up. I will always believe I am a living, breathing, walking, talking, miracle of God and a witness for many to show God's healing power. It's astounding how the power of God works, me giving my testimony of 'my miracle,' and then Bishop teaching on John 11 recounting the death of Lazarus and 'his miracle' of Jesus raising him from the dead. He gave a powerful teaching that night, and I realized his dedication and commitment to the commission that Jesus gave. Go out and preach the gospel to all for the kingdom of God is at hand.

Bishop is selfless in doing that commission. He and his wife drive for three hours from Poplar Bluff Missouri to Springfield Missouri and three hours back again every Monday. It doesn't matter if there are 3 or 30 people in the sanctuary, he is there every Monday to preach and teach the good news of our Lord. This isn't to lift up

Bishop, but to show his faithfulness and obedience of how we must all exalt God first and give Him all the Glory. At the end of the service, several people approached the altar for prayer. All were seeking God's will for some situation going on in their lives. Each one that came to the altar had been fasting for 21 days. Twenty-one days! That shows their perseverance in seeking God's face and getting an answer for their need.

There was a very sweet spirit among those in the congregation that night. You could feel it. Bishop preceded to go from person-to-person praying and laying hands on them. My husband leaned over and said to me, "See what's going on up there at the altar? That's what went on in your room when he came to see you in the hospital." I looked at him, smiled and giggled with joy, a joy that comes only from God. I then asked, "Did the nurses and staff see all of it?" "Oh yes" he replied, and it carried right out into the hallway." "I love it!" I exclaimed, "Praise God!"

It was a regular old-time revival, and it is so needed for the times we are living in. That was the first time I heard about what happened when Bishop Webb came to pray for me while I was in the hospital. Bishop later told me, "I knew you could hear me. You were moving, and your feet were removing you were responding." I pray all who heard him that night were touched by the Lord, and their needs were met, and that they took the blessings of that night to others to be touched. I also appreciated the worship leader and told her so that night. She chose to sing many of the old hymns and those pertaining to "The Blood of Jesus." For without the shedding of the blood by Jesus there is no Christianity. As the old hymn says "What can wash my sins away? Nothing, but the Blood of Jesus." Without the blood, there is no redemption for sin. Jesus was the final sacrifice on the cross for the redemption of our sins by shedding His blood for all the world. All you need to do is receive that gift and believe and know He died for you.

CHAPTER 4

TWO REALITIES

It is amazing how the mind works when you are in a sedated condition. It is almost as if you are experiencing things in two different worlds. The real world that corresponds with what's actually happening, and the world in your mind that feels like your actually experiencing these strange events, but you're not. You become disoriented and start to create things in your mind. Your last point of reference is your last memory. As we now look back, there were several comical moments that we can see the humor in now, which we can all laugh about.

For example, like the time when I told Sally, my husband, Jim left me in Springfield. He just left me there! I tried to use someone's phone to call her to come and get me, but when she arrived they wouldn't let her in, so she left. Or one day when my husband Jim came to visit, I saw he dyed his hair purple. In my mind, I was convinced he really had purple hair. I remember telling him, "Honey you really don't look good in purple hair you need to take it out." He just held my hand and gently said, "Okay sweetheart I'll do that." We can now laugh about it, but at the time I thought I was actually experiencing these things. They were as real as real could be. The funny thing about being sedated is that you have no idea about what is actually happening in your life at that time. I did not understand that I was sick, or that I was even in the hospital. I kept thinking I was some kind of prisoner being tied up and held against my will keeping me away from my family. Well in a way that was true, but they certainly weren't mean people and I had to be in the hospital at the time.

My husband would later tell me three times I was told, "Now Lisa don't pull the tube out of your mouth because it has to be there to help you, okay?" I would shake my head "yes" I was told, and then try to remove all the tubes again. I don't even remember anyone telling me that. The nurses did end up having to restrain my hands for a little while so I wouldn't cause great harm to myself. Although your mind tells you these strange and unusual things are happening. Like there was an Italian restaurant down the hall in the hospital with a statue of Mussolini that stood outside the restaurant. Why I thought there was an Italian restaurant in the hospital with a statue of Mussolini outside of it, I will never know.

My husband and son came to the hospital to be with me on Thanksgiving. But of course, I had no idea it was the day of Thanksgiving. All I kept saying was, "I have to go home so I can cook Thanksgiving dinner." The last thing I knew was my brother and sister-in-law would be there for Thanksgiving. Jim would say, "Its okay. You don't have to worry about dinner." Our son was so very supportive every time he would come and see me he would reassure his father by saying, "Moms going to be just fine. Everything is going to be fine." And of course, his Dad would always agree. Your last point of reference is your last memory. You have no idea about anything you are actually experiencing at the moment.

The one thing that I will always remember is there was a nurse who was blond with a bob haircut. I thought she was such a sweet person. I said to her, "I hope you can know the Son of Man someday." She looked at me with an odd look. Then I asked her, "Can I have something to write with, like a pad of paper?" She gave it to me, and I wrote "John 3:16." She said, "No one has ever said this to me. I never heard of this before. What does it mean?" I responded, "Look it up in the Bible. Read it, John 3:16." That was how I saw it in my mind and how I experienced it while sedated. What actually happened was said to me later by my husband, Jim. There was a nurse who was blond with a bob haircut, and I did ask to write, but what I wrote was just gobbledygook. Then I wrote something as clear as a bell. I wrote "John 3:16." I wrote it several times over and over again "John 3:16," and it was the only thing I wrote that you could make out. I remember saying to Jim, "So I really wrote John 3:16?" "Yes you did" he replied. I then asked "And all of the nurses and staff saw it? Did they know and understand what it meant?" He answered, "Some did, but everyone saw it, and it was quiet."

And as for the little blond nurse with a bob haircut, I did see her as I got better and stronger in the ICU. One night I said something to her about God, and she said, "Oh yeah, the Bible and that verse you gave me." I thought, "Well, something did happen," and hopefully that conversation prompted her to read the Bible and to discover who the Son of Man really is.

CHAPTER 5

GOD WAS ALWAYS WITH ME

The first thing I remember upon waking up and being in the ICU was my dear friend Sally and two other wonderful friends from our church standing next to my bed. I can remember being so thirsty at the time because I had nothing to drink for days when I was only given sponges to suck on. The surgeon came in and said I could have a little water. The nurse then gave me a cup of ice cold water, and it was the best thing I had ever tasted in my life. This was the first memory that I actually had from being in the ambulance, arriving at the hospital, and the first encounter I had with the emergency room doctor. I was as weak as a kitten, and my long road to recovery had just begun. Looking back now it wasn't as long as it could've been for God's hand and His intervention was in that as well.

From the moment I was awake and aware in the ICU, I knew God was going to shield, protect, and heal me. There never was a question in my mind. I knew it! I was being healed through divine intervention by prayer because of faith. God always provides answers to all things in His word.

In the Bible, there are 50+ verses in Scripture that God uses to initiate His healing power for us. His name is Jehovah-Rapha (more appropriately Yahweh-Rapha): "The Lord who heals" in Hebrew. Here are several of those promises God gave us:

- "... If you diligently heed the voice of the LORD your God and do what is right in His sight, give ear to His commandments and keep all His statutes, I will put none of the diseases on you which I have brought on the Egyptians. For I am the LORD who heals you" —Exodus 15:26 (NKJV)

- "...And I will take sickness away from the midst of you. ...I will fulfill the number of your days." —Exodus 23:25-26 (NKJV)

- "Heal me, O LORD, and I shall be healed; Save me, and I shall be saved, For You are my praise." — Jeremiah 17:14 (NKJV)

- Thus says the LORD,... I have heard your prayer, I have seen your tears; surely I will heal you.— 2 Kings 20:5 (NKJV)

- "His flesh shall be young like a child's, He shall return to the days of his youth. He shall pray to God, and He will delight in him, He shall see His face with joy, for He restores to man His righteousness."— Job 33:25-26 (NKJV)

- "O LORD my God, I cried out to You, And You healed me."— Psalms 30:2 (NKJV)

- Bless the LORD, O my soul, And forget not all His benefits: Who forgives all your iniquities Who heals all your diseases, Who redeems your life from destruction, Who crowns you with lovingkindness and tender mercies, —Psalms 103:2-4 (NKJV)

- ...But the tongue of the wise promotes health. — Proverbs 12:18 (NKJV)

- But to you who fear My name The Sun of Righteousness shall arise with healing in His wings; And you shall go out... — Malachi 4:2 (NKJV)

- "They will take up serpents; and if they drink anything deadly, it will by no means hurt them; they will lay hands on the sick, and they will recover."— Mark 16:18 (NKJV)

- "But when the multitudes knew it, they followed Him; and He received them and spoke to them about the kingdom of God, and healed those who have need of healing"— Luke 9:11 (NKJV)

- "And he laid his hands on her: and immediately she was made straight, and glorified God ... And ought not this woman, being a daughter of Abraham, whom Satan hath bound, lo, these 18 years, be loosed from his bond on the Sabbath day? — Luke 13:16 (KJV)

- "How God anointed Jesus of Nazareth with the Holy Ghost and with power, who went about doing good and healing all who were oppressed of the devil, for God was with him — Acts 10:38 (KJV)

- "But He was wounded for our transgressions, He was bruised for our iniquities;

The chastisement for our peace was upon Him, and by His stripes we are healed." — Isaiah 53:5 (NKJV)

- "... And pray for one another, that you may be healed. The effective, fervent prayer of a righteous man of avails much."— James 5:16 (NKJV)

- "Who Himself bore our sins in His own body on the tree, that we, having died to sins, might live for righteousness-by whose stripes you were healed"—1 Peter 2:24 (NKJV)

- "Beloved, I pray that you may prosper in all things and be in health, just as your soul prospers." — 3 John 2 (NKJV)

It is documented in three out of the four Gospels that Jesus Himself declares "I am willing be cleansed" or (be healed). Here are the Scriptures where this is found:

- Then Jesus put out His hand and touched him, saying,"I am willing; be cleansed." Immediately his leprosy was cleansed.— Matthew 8:3 (NKJV)

- Then Jesus, moved with compassion, stretched out His hand and touched him, and said to him, "I am willing; be cleansed."—Mark 1:41 (NKJV)

- Then He put out His hand and touched him, saying, "I am willing; be cleansed." Immediately the leprosy left him.— Luke 5:13 (NKJV)

One of the best scriptures that depicts Jesus as the Son of God and His great commission is in Matthew. It perfectly demonstrates Jesus being the great physician and mighty healer while teaching the gospel that ultimately points to the kingdom:

- "And Jesus went about all Galilee, teaching in their synagogues, preaching the gospel of the kingdom, and healing all kinds of sickness and all kinds of disease among the people." — Matthew 4:23 (NKJV)

One of the biggest lies Satan uses to deceive people with is that they are sick and feeble and nothing can be done. It is a lie that keeps people in bondage and unable to attain their destiny that God has put forth for their lives. We are to be a light in the world, and we must do it in good health. The hardest thing for people to learn when they are going through some sort of situation is to not keep talking about it. They keep putting it out in the atmosphere, 'how sick they are' and 'how they don't feel well.' That is the worst thing you could possibly do. Even if you don't feel well, even if something is going on with your body you have to bind those words and speak 'healing' in the atmosphere. The power is in the 'tongue.' We must always remember that. Keep in mind, God spoke the world into existence, and we must never forget it. "For He spoke, and it was done; he commanded, and it stood fast" Psalm-33:9 (KJV). Always remember what we speak shall come forth in our lives.

CHAPTER 6

THE LORD IS MY STRENGTH

The first time the physical therapist or PT came to my room and got me out of my bed and to my feet was absolutely hilarious. The PT, with her assistant, had me sit up and dangle my feet over the side of the bed. Then they held the walker steady as I pushed up using my arms to get to my feet. I fell back onto the bed with the first try, but then after a few more attempts, I got to my feet. As they held on to me, I stood there and just wobbled back and forth. It felt as if all of my insides were going to fall out. It was a strange feeling and an odd sensation. I would continue to have that odd sensation for almost the entire time I was in the hospital. I couldn't control my feet or my legs, they just twitched and moved, and I just stood there and laughed. My PT was so kind as she commented, "A lot of people would like to dance like that." I replied, "Yeah, it's like I have crazy legs." She laughed as she said, "That's a good name for that new dance. Crazy legs!" Little did she know that I had been a dancer for most of my life, as well as being a dance teacher and choreographer. My first walk was basically just around my room which wasn't very large. I used a walker, and I had the 'big belt' around me with my physical therapist guiding each step. The big belt or giant belt is a device used by physical therapists to assist patients having problems with balance. It actually is a big belt.

Later that afternoon my mind went to prayer as I thought, "Lord, You blessed me with the most precious gift of dance, for I always knew that it was a God-given talent." I looked up at the ceiling of my hospital room and laughed as I said, "Being an award-winning choreographer that was easy, but walking, now that's hard." I then realized I was the dance student and God was my choreographer. He meticulously arranged each step of this new dance I had never danced before. I just needed to master each step and follow His lead. I then sighed and whispered, "But-God." With each new day, the PT would come with her assistant, and they were always cheerful and encouraging. I started to be able to walk through the halls, but it was extremely tiring because I basically had no energy in the beginning. A couple of times I would have to stop and sit in a chair that an aide followed me with before I could continue on, and of course, I had to use a walker. There were days when she wouldn't come, and I was so disappointed because I wanted to continue my progress.

One of the biggest struggles I had during that time was not having an appetite and my stomach being so small from not eating for such an extended period of time. I was still being fed intravenously and had just started on liquids upon arriving in the ICU. The surgeon wanted to start me on solids, but when I tried food, I thought I would gag. It was a constant struggle. But it just so happened that on one of those difficult days, a dear couple from our church came to visit me. She brought a lovely Christmas mug filled with fresh evergreens. The delightful scent of pine filled my hospital room, and it was lovely. They prayed with me and encouraged me. And we talked about the strength of the Lord. That's when I started to quote on a daily basis, "I can do all things through Christ who strengthens me" Philippians 4:13 (NKJV). We must come to the realization that it isn't just a bunch of words on a piece of paper. It is actual 'power.' It is strength through Him and He alone. Jesus generates the source of healing to our body. The Bible is the 'word' of God. These are not just mere words written in a book, they are life-giving words. They are essential to our healing for they are words of 'power' and 'life.' My thoughts would continually turn to the Lord. These words of healing were pivotal and became my source of strength. And with each passing day, I persevered and did become stronger.

Strength is essential for any recovery. If we look to the Bible, we can discover many Scriptures that encourage us in regaining our strength. Here are but a few:

- "Fear thou not; for I am with thee: be not dismayed for I am thy God; I will strengthen thee; yea, I will help thee; yea I will uphold thee with the right hand of my righteousness"— Isaiah 41:10 (KJV)

- "But they that wait upon the LORD shall renew their strength; they shall mount up with wings as eagles; they shall run, and not be weary; and they shall walk, and not faint."— Isaiah 40:31 (KJV)

- "My flesh and my heart faileth; but God is the strength of my heart, and my portion forever." —Psalm 73:26 (KJV)

- "Seek the LORD and his strength; seek his face continually."— 1 Chronicles 16:11 (KJV)

- "I will love thee, O LORD my strength, The LORD is my rock, and my fortress, and my deliverer; my God, my strength, in whom I will trust; my buckler, and the horn of my salvation, and my high tower." — Psalm 18:1-2 (KJV)

- "Watch ye, stand fast in the faith, quit you like men, be strong." —1 Corinthians 16:13(KJV)

- "The LORD God is my strength, and he will make my feet like hinds' feet, and he will make me walk upon mine high places. To the chief singer on my stringed instruments."— Habakkuk 3:19 (KJV)

- "And thou shalt love the Lord thy God with all thy heart, and with all thy soul, and with all thy mind, and with all thy strength: this is the first commandment." — Mark 12:30 (KJV)

It doesn't matter the situation we may go through in our life. Whatever crisis or problem that occurs. For we always have the confidence in knowing we have the support of Almighty God and all the answers we need are continually found in the word of God.

CHAPTER 7

GOD HAD US IN JUST THE RIGHT PLACE

My stay in the hospital was a lengthy one. But I was in just the right place getting the best quality of care that is available. The expertise of the surgeons and medical staff was crucial for my recovery, and I received the highest level of medical care. God had me at one of the top-ranking hospitals in Missouri, with the top-ranking surgical group in Springfield. Yes, God had me at the right place at the right time. My husband Jim who had retired in Michigan had just started a part-time job a couple of weeks prior to all of this happening. Our son was in the eighth grade, and we wouldn't leave him alone. We had to make sure he got to and from school and to all activities he was involved in. This would've been quite an undertaking for one person, that being my husband, Jim. But God! Again, my heavenly Father Yahweh Intervened. He had us right in the right place, at the right time, with the right people. From the surgeons and medical staff at the hospital to the wonderful people that surrounded us near our home.

As always my friend Sally was so generous and helpful, but also there was the mom of my son's best friend, who stepped up and was very supportive. She was continually there when most needed and always ready to help. I stand in awe of how God's hand was in every detail. Having people that were so helpful and loyal being there when things really got bad.

Being in the hospital in Springfield, meant that I was about an hour away from our home. Jim would try to come up before or after work, all the while taking care of our son by doing the grocery shopping, cooking, cleaning, and laundry. If he couldn't pick our son up from school, Sally was right there taking him to one of his favorite fast food restaurants, and then to her home if needed. He also would go home with his best friend and spend time with her and always have a home cooked meal if Jim had to work late. All of these acts of kindness were so gracious and would've been more than enough, but amazingly it didn't stop there. Even the principal at the school had a special pizza party set up for my son and his friend one day after school.

Upon my arriving home from the hospital, there was a steady flow of generosity with people from our church bringing lovely meals and spending time with me during the day. I was unable to attend my son's Christmas concert at school, for I still was very weak. He was going to be singing a solo. This was very disappointing to me, but again many of our friends stepped up and were more than willing to take him to the concert, cheer him on, and bring him home. The outpouring of kindness from the people in the Ozarks where we now live and make our home was remarkable. I will always treasure their thoughtfulness and the memory of what they did.

CHAPTER 8

TIME IS SHORT

My room in the hospital was in a perfect location. The front of it was all windows with sliding glass doors that were often left open. It was in front of the nurses' station and had a kitchenette off to the side where the staff could get breakfast and have snacks. Throughout the day I watched as people were coming and going to the kitchenette, and I would see each shift change at the nurses' station.

I remember one particular evening that was very strange. There was a breach of the security system which caused the lights to flash on and off continually followed by sirens and announcements. It was very odd. I remember seeing a flurry of activity with the normal hustle and bustle being intensified as the staff went back and forth and many things that were said. That's when I really realized how much God is in control. I laid there and watched the activity through the windows and open glass doors and thought "I don't have to worry or be afraid because Jesus is always with me. If He has brought me this far through all I have gone through, I know by His authority that Jesus has this." The authority that Jesus has entrusted us with can deal with any situation. I knew I was in the palm of His hand and no ill would come to me.

On that same night, a man was wheeled past my room on a hospital bed. I heard him say, "Oh my God I think I'm going to die tonight." I immediately thought and said out loud, "Dear God let him know You, all he has to do is ask." I later found out that man did end up dying that same night. There was a funeral and service about a day later in the hospital. I thought that was very peculiar at the time. I had remembered seeing and hearing bits of conversation that indicated he was a veteran. Maybe he didn't have a lot of family or friends. It made me really start to think how sad it would be to be in his position, knowing that you were dying, if you didn't know Jesus as your Savior. I recalled seeing that same man a few days earlier walking the halls. There were a couple of people with him that were encouraging him and took video, but now he was gone. Later, my husband would tell me that there were a couple of people who passed away while I was in the ICU. I knew of one of them.

This is why we must always be ready by having our hearts pure before the Lord. Life is fragile and short. We must be prepared to see the face of God and stand before Him. You only have two options. To be saved and be with the Lord, or to die lost and be in eternal damnation. It sounds very harsh. I understand. But it is 'our reality.' All you need to do is recognize and believe in your heart that Jesus is the Son of God. That He died for you to forgive your sins, and receive the gift of eternal life, to be saved. Time is very short. We must always be ready.

CHAPTER 9

TAKING THE NEXT BIG STEP

I waited for days to get a room and leave the ICU ward. As you start to get better, you no longer need the help from machines to support your body, nor do you need to be continuously monitored. This can be a stressful time for patients because there is no longer the one-on-one nursing that there was in the early stages, but you are still far from being well. In this new level of care as you move to this new ward, there will be a written plan that includes; a summary of your care and treatment while you were in the ICU, a monitoring plan to make sure you continue to recover, a plan for ongoing treatment and details of your physical rehabilitation needs. It took my surgeon about three to four days before finally securing a room on one of these other floors. It was December and so many people were leaving the ICU and transferring to another ward in the hospital with a reduced level of care. This is the first step in the process of going home. As I said, it took a few days before I was able to move to the next level. Every day starting from December 1st I would ask "Is there a room available yet?" and the answer would be, "Not yet, but there should be one be very soon." Finally, on December 4th I got a room and left the ICU. I was ecstatic! The nurse came into the room with a wheelchair and assisted me to the elevator and up to the next level of care I went. There was a little miscommunication about the IV that was still feeding me intravenously. The orders were not given to remove it that morning, so up I went with the IV securely in place.

The whole time I had been in the ICU I had an IV pole, a urine bag for I was still using a catheter, still experiencing the sensation of my insides falling out, and so weak that I could hardly make it around using a walker. Those first days in the ICU were extremely taxing and difficult, but I tried to walk and move as much as I could even though all of these devices were inhibiting me. The catheter was removed around the last day of November, and I started the process of getting up, with assistance, and urinating by myself. This was a huge event in itself. I had a catheter for all those weeks, and now my body had to readjust.

One of the best things I experienced that first day on the reduced care floor was a wonderful shower and having my hair washed. It was absolute heaven. For weeks I only had sponge baths, and my hair hadn't been washed until then. Finally, I could take a proper shower and it felt so good. I had two wonderful nurses that assisted me. They made sure the stoma site was covered so as not to get it wet. And I still had a picc line in place. A picc line is placed into a large vein in your arm and guides the catheter up into the main vein near your heart where blood flows quickly. The line was left in place just as a precaution in the event of an emergency, and the nurses thoroughly covered that as well. As I sat in the shower chair, they thoroughly bathed me from head to toe, and I felt totally refreshed. There were so many knots in my hair that it took one nurse literally 5 to 10 minutes trying not to pull my hair while gingerly combing them out. Those two ladies were so kind and helpful in assisting me in my first bath that helped to set me on the road to my recovery.

I was in a single room in the ICU. Now I would be in a double room and share it with a roommate. The room that they brought me to had a woman who was very unhappy about being there. She started banging on things, constantly calling the nurse and just being downright ornery. I thought, "Please Lord I've got to talk to the nurse. I'll never be able to get any sleep tonight." The nurse came in and after finishing with my roommate walked around to my side and whispered, "We have another room for you. We'll be moving you shortly." "Oh thank you so much," I said to the nurse. "Thank God," I said to myself. What an answer to prayer, for I never would've gotten any rest in that room. Before I could even ask her the situation was taken care of. Praise God!

My friend Sally was the first one to see me on my new floor and level. My eyes were closed when she arrived. I opened them, and there she was with that big smile. She was standing there holding the most beautiful red poinsettia. I was so happy to see her, and she had brought her daughter with her. We all chatted about how well I was doing, and they asked about Jim and my son. They stayed for a while, but as quick as they came off they were again on their way to a Christmas party. The nurses came just as promised and moved me to the new room. It was absolutely lovely and I was in a single room again. Jim was there as they moved me and it felt so good to have him there. My dinner was soon to arrive, and I was thrilled to be eating real food again. The head nurse came in and told me that they were going to remove the IV at 6 o'clock that evening. They did! Right on time at 6 o'clock sharp the nurse came in and removed the IV. "There you go your free" she laughed. Now I could finally relax and enjoy my meal. Jim was telling me all the news of the day from back home, and I felt such peace for I knew all was well. Before long I started to drift off to sleep with sweet dreams of having all of this behind me. At last, I knew I would be ready to go home.

Being on this floor was certainly a challenge. I was still very fatigued and would try as hard as I could to walk and move, but some days I just felt exhausted. After having such a caring PT in the ICU ward, the one that I had on this floor was entirely different. Let's just say her bedside manner leaves much to be desired. It was not quite what it should be, and her attitude instead of being encouraging was demanding and in a way belittling. I can honestly say that this encounter was not the norm, for most of the medical staff was absolutely wonderful. I can remember it was on the third day being on that floor when she came in and said "Now, I want you to set up, get out of bed, and put your socks on. I looked at her like she was crazy and proceeded to try to do as she said. Of course, it didn't happen. Then she said "We're going to go for a walk, but you're not going to use a walker. We'll use the big belt. It'll be fine." "O...kay..." I said slowly, still looking at her like she was nuts. "It'll be fine" she reassured me. So off we went with the big belt in place for our walk down the hallway.

This must've been quite a sight. The PT was holding me from behind using the big belt, and me weaving back and forth, back and forth like a drunken sailor all the way down the hallway. I started to laugh, "I have absolutely no control over my body or where it's going," I said as I continued to laugh. "I couldn't walk a straight line if you paid me," I said still laughing. Then she said to me "You're breathing through your mouth not breathing through your nose. You have to breathe through your nose. You have to breathe and step, breathe and step. Now do that as you go down the hallway." So I started to do as she said. Breathe and step, breathe and step. It sounded like a bad dance routine, breathe and step. About halfway down the hallway I needed to stop and I leaned against the wall. "I think I need to go back now," I said with shortness in my breath. She huffed, "Are you sure?" "Yep, pretty sure" I answered. She begrudgingly led me back to my room, weaving back and forth all the way.

When we got to the room, I sat in the recliner. I was sitting up for most of the day now, and only using the bed to sleep in at night. I made an effort to do this myself. She then said before leaving "You're going to have to do better than this if you want to go home." I just smiled as she left the room and thought, "Dear God get me out of here." Again God's grace was upon me.

I took it upon myself to walk at least three times a day. I would make it a point to catch a nurse every time one was in my room. I would say "Can we go for a walk?" And usually, they would say "Sure." Or sometimes they would tell me they would be back later. Either way I did my walking, and of course, it was charted. I showed improvement each day and before long I was on my way home.

I thought about that experience after getting back home and prayed for that PT. I couldn't really say the words, so I prayed in the Spirit and gave it to the Lord, for I wasn't going to hang on to those hurtful feelings any longer. I can now look back and even laugh about many of the things she said and did. I can honestly say I wish her well. Now being only a distant memory, I can see it was just another stepping stone in my journey home.

Another major challenge I faced was my oxygen saturation levels were only in the 80% levels. This is quite low because they should be in the high 90% levels to be in the normal range. One of the nurses after taking my vitals decided to put me on a small amount of oxygen. This was helpful at the time but would be detrimental in trying to go home. There was no real reason for me to be on oxygen, and they did not want to okay an oxygen tank for me upon being discharged. I really didn't need it, but I was having some breathing issues.

From the very beginning of my stay in the hospital, the respiratory therapist recommended I do exercises both in the hospital and at home. The concern is always with pneumonia. The reason behind this is after abdominal surgery breathing and coughing can suddenly become painful and difficult. I was told to hold a pillow at my abdomen if I needed to cough. They also gave me this small handheld device, technically called, a Breath Builder Volumetric. Upon receiving this device I remembered my mother having to do the same thing many years before when she was in the hospital. This breath builder is standard practice in most hospitals. She had great difficulty using it, and at that moment,

I was no different. It was so hard for me to try to suck in and lift the ball. I would faithfully do it every day, several times a day, but I couldn't even get up to 500 or 1000. My surgeon would come in every day and have me 'try it again' and would just shake his head in disbelief that I couldn't achieve this small task. It wasn't small to me. It was monumental! But God's hand was about to intervene again. The mystery of having such low oxygen saturation levels was soon to be revealed, and I thank God every day for what He was about to do.

CHAPTER 10

CAN I GO HOME YET?

Whenever the surgeon came into my room, I hoped, "Oh please let this be the day that he tells me I can go home tomorrow," but for a long time that day didn't come. I really like my surgeon, but I was experiencing a love-hate relationship with him for a while. Don't get me wrong, he is an accomplished surgeon, but he is meticulous. Looking back now I am so thankful and grateful to God that I had such a cautious and accomplished surgeon. If there was one little thing that didn't quite settle with him, he would think about it, and think about it, until he really knew which direction he wanted to take. This actually helped numerous times and led to me having several procedures that proved beneficial and set me on the road to my recovery.

One example of this was before I moved to the reduced level of care floor in the hospital, and the surgeon called for an MRI. He wanted to make sure everything was healing as it should. The MRI confirmed all was well and healing, but it also showed a very small area in my right lung that had fluid on it. He decided to schedule a procedure known as a Thoracentesis. This procedure is done by inserting a needle into the pleural space between the lungs and the chest wall. This condition is known as a pleural effusion where there is excess fluid in the lungs and causes difficulty in breathing. The pleural space is the small space between the lungs and the chest wall. The goal is to drain the fluid making it easier to breathe again. The amount of fluid drained varies depending on the reason, and it typically takes 10 to 15 minutes, but it can take longer if there's a lot of fluid in the pleural space. It ended up being that tiny area of fluid in my right lung had 2 liters of fluid that would be removed. No wonder my breathing was so impaired and restricted the flow of oxygen into my lungs causing saturation levels to be so low. The doctor doing the procedure explained, "You might start to cough right after I'm finished. This is absolutely normal and a very good sign." I did start to cough, and the more I coughed, phlegm started to loosen and began to come up. I felt great! I took a deep breath, and I couldn't believe how much air I could take in.

Later that day after the procedure I saw my surgeon and commented to him, "You don't know how bad you feel until you know what it feels like to feel good." I didn't know how ill I was because it had become normal to me. It wasn't until I started feeling good that I could see just how sick I really was. The only explanation for the spot on my lung was that I had a huge amount of fluid pumped into my body while I was septic, and some may have spilled into the chest wall. Or it just could've been another layer of the underlying illness that I was experiencing during that time. As for the breathing exercises that I was to do with my handheld device, well guess what? I was able to do them better than ever. When I got home, I went up to the 1500 mark that my surgeon so wanted me to achieve while in the hospital. When I came home after my second surgery, I could go up to 2500 and beyond without even batting an eyelash. The mystery had been solved, and again God was victorious!

Once again Providence was responsible for all that was revealed. Providence- being the hand of God. If I hadn't had the MRI to check on my surgery, they wouldn't have seen the tiny spot on my right lung, and if they hadn't seen the tiny spot on my right lung, they wouldn't have drained 2 liters of fluid off of my lung which ultimately made my breathing 100% normal again. And without fail, all of this brings us right back to the Bible that holds all the answers for our lives. What is God's will for my life? We find the answer in Jeremiah and Mark.

- "For I know the thoughts that I think toward you, says the LORD, thoughts of peace and not of evil, to give you a future and a hope."—Jeremiah 29:11 (NKJV)

God is clear by saying 'His thoughts' are towards 'us' and He wants nothing less than for us to have a perfect 'future' and 'hope.'

- "For whoever does the will of God, is My brother and My sister and mother." — Mark 3:35 (NKJV)

Jesus Himself spoke these words, and it shows how we become the family of God and become joint heirs as sons and daughters of His kingdom.

God's desire for His children is never to be weak and feeble. We are to be worshipers and to give thanks in all things as we come to the throne. 1 Thessalonians 5:18 ..." give thanks in all circumstances; for this is God's will for you in Christ Jesus." (NIV). Perfect health with gratitude, in giving thanks, and having a grateful heart is all part of God's will for our lives for those who have Jesus Christ in their heart. For there lies the promise in 1 John 2:17: "And the world is passing away, and the lust of it; but he who does the will of God abides forever." (NKJV). This is God's promise. This is God's will. If we abide and do His will we have the precious gift of eternal life through His Son Jesus Christ. God wants always to give us a 'perfect future' and a 'perfect goal leading towards our desired hope.' This is the plan and the path God lays out for our lives. It's up to us to follow His plan and fulfill God's destiny for us as He intended.

CHAPTER 11

DISCERNING THE SIGNS OF OUR TIMES

I heard the exciting news while still in the hospital that President Donald Trump announced the United States recognition of Jerusalem as the capital of Israel, and ordered the planning of the relocation of the U.S. Embassy from Tel Aviv to Jerusalem. Several other Presidents had made the same promise, but it was President Trump, being a man of his word that actually did it. The psalmist David speaks on this very issue where God's stand is unmovable! "Pray for the peace of Jerusalem; they shall prosper that love thee." Psalm 122:6 (KJV). The Jewish people had taken back Jerusalem in 1967 during the six-day war, and now, finally, it is being recognized just in time for the 70th anniversary of Israel becoming a nation on May 14 as the capital of Israel. I was euphoric! I wanted to run around the whole hospital shouting with joy! There is so much going on in our world today. Current events that are prophetic are being fulfilled right before our very eyes. Without question, I have come to the realization that we are absolutely living in the last days by seeing such marvelous events unfold before us. But I also believe the end of the 'church age' and the last days actually started over 100 years ago.

With the establishment of Zionism under the leadership of Theodore Herzl in 1897, and the Balfour declaration of 1917, which continued the Zionist movement with the British returning the land to the Jewish people taking it out of the hands of the Ottoman Empire who dominated the region for over 400 years. Then across the decades to the year 1948 with President Harry Truman recognizing Israel as a nation and fulfilling the prophecy of 'a nation being born in a day', to the present year of 2017 when President Donald Trump declared once and for all that Jerusalem, as it always has been, and will be, the capital of Israel. So the claim could be made that we are actually in the last days of the last days.

The word of God tells us in Genesis 1:14 He will use the sun, moon, and stars "for signs and seasons, and for days and years" (NKJV) revealing significant events. This was proven when the Revelation 12 constellation appeared in the sky a few months before President Trump announced the U.S. recognition of Jerusalem as the capital of Israel. Is God sending a message to those who have 'eyes to see?' The High Holy Days of Rosh Hashanah in Judaism began at sundown on September 20th and ended with nightfall September 22nd. Then, the Revelation 12 constellation appeared on September 23rd. Yom Kippur, the second most sacred day of the year in Judaism ended the month of September beginning on the evening of the 29th and ending the evening of the 30th. A few months after that on December 6th President Trump announced his support in recognizing Jerusalem as the capital of Israel. All of these dates consecutively occurred during the same year of 2017. Could God be speaking with few actually understanding and hearing what He is saying? Study Revelation 12 for yourself. It is essential that Christians study and understand their Judeo-Christian roots.

Although, with all the good news there is also bad. There are heinous crimes and people with hateful rhetoric that are ripping apart our country. Natural disasters are occurring at an alarming rate. The fires in California, the hurricanes that hit Houston Texas, and Florida, the volcanic eruptions in Hawaii and Guatemala, and mega earthquakes most recently in Venezuela and off the island of Fiji are but a few signs that Jesus warned us about as we approach the last days. I started to think about how events-good and bad- are happening at warp speed on this earth. The Scripture came to mind about the cares of this world. In Mark 4:19-20 it says "... and the cares of this world, the deceitfulness of riches, and the desires for other things entering in choke the word, and it becomes unfruitful. But these are the ones sown on good ground, those who hear the word, accept it, and bear fruit: some thirtyfold, some sixty, and some a hundred" (NKJV).

We must have 'eyes to see' and 'ears to hear.' For only then will we know the truth, bear good fruit, and promote the outpouring of the Holy Spirit advancing the spread of the gospel and the kingdom. We must always bear good fruit and never allow the cares of this world to 'choke the word' in us. It can be the best of times or the worst of times depending on your stand and acknowledgment of Jesus as your Lord and Savior. He is our true Redeemer. And what we reap shall be thirty-fold, sixty-fold or even hundred-fold, depending on our steadfastness and commitment to the Lord. We can never do enough to 'advance the gospel' and 'promote the outpouring of the Holy Spirit.' Jesus is the way, the truth, and the life. No man comes to the Father except through Him. God will reward us, with many crowns for taking a stand. It's all about our stand, our loyalty, and our commitment to the 'word,' for Jesus is the 'word!'

In Luke 9:23 Then He said to them all, " If anyone desires to come after Me, let him deny himself, and take up his cross daily, and follow Me" (NKJV). He also said in Luke 11:33-36 "No one, when he has lit a lamp, puts it in a secret place or under a basket, but on the lampstand, that those who come in may see the light. The lamp of the body is the eye. Therefore, when your eye is good, your whole body also is full of light. But when your eye is bad, your body also is full of darkness. Therefore take heed that the light which is in you is not darkness. If then your whole body is full of light, having no part dark, the whole body will be full of light, as when the bright shining of a lamp gives you light" (NKJV). Again, this speaks to us about our life being a 'light to the world' and not being concerned with the troubles or cares of this world. We must guard our heart, our mind, and our eyes from all things that are dark or evil. We must always look toward God who is the 'ultimate light.' If we keep our eyes pure then, our body will be pure. And our body is the temple of the Holy

Spirit. We are to be 'lights' and spread the gospel of the kingdom for as long as we have on this earth. For the time is short and prophetic events are progressing rapidly. Be aware and be ready!

CHAPTER 12

HOME FOR CHRISTMAS

At long last, the day finally arrived when I could go home. I wanted to be home more than anything. I waited with anticipation, as each hour passed by. It was December 9th, exactly 3 weeks and three days from when I enter the hospital. That particular day also happened to be my birthday. I was still in the hospital at lunchtime when the cafeteria sent up a little tiny piece of cake along with a birthday card on my tray. I thought it was the sweetest gesture, so kind and thoughtful. The server even sang "Happy Birthday" as he brought the tray into my room. Naturally, being in the hospital on my birthday was not my first choice, but that act of kindness, being discharged, and going home was the best present I could have had.

I ended up being discharged in the early evening. The nurse practitioner for the cardiologist had been in that afternoon and advised the surgeon that I should be on a low dose beta blocker for my blood pressure, and heart rate was slightly elevated. I left the hospital that night with a prescription for a beta blocker, an iron pill, and an antibiotic. All 3 things I had not been on before and was hoping to be off as soon as I had recuperated at home. The biggest thing I went home with was a colostomy bag, technically known as, a colostomy pouching system.

This was indeed a life-altering experience, which would only be temporary. I knew a dear woman, back in Michigan when I was in my teens and early 20s that had experienced a colostomy and had a bag for years. It puts into perspective what she went through now that I am experiencing the same thing. She too eventually had reversal surgery, but it was years after she initially had her colostomy. For all the men and women that live daily with a colostomy, I genuinely share empathy for their courage and discipline. As each day passed, I became more accustomed to having a colostomy and dealing with the bag. It even started to become more like second nature. Through all of it, even at my lowest point, I knew all was for good. I would tell myself Rejoice! I knew I was in the middle of God's love and the enemy's hate. My God is gracious and controls all things, so again I say Rejoice! Keep in mind all things work for good, for those who love the Lord. Paul speaks on a similar issue in the Bible. He describes having "a thorn in the flesh:"

- ...Therefore, in order to keep me from becoming conceited, I was given a thorn in my flesh, a messenger of Satan, to torment me. Three times I pleaded with the Lord to take it away from me. But He said to me, "My grace is sufficient for you, for my power is made perfect in weakness." Therefore I will boast all the more gladly about my weaknesses, so that Christ's power may rest on me. That is why, for Christ's sake, I delight in weaknesses, in insults, in hardships, in persecutions, in difficulties. For when I am weak, then I am strong. — 2 Corinthians 12:7-10 (NIV)

There are different teachings out today of what exactly was the thorn in Paul's flesh. Some think it was spiritual, others believe it was physical. Either way, you can study the Scriptures and decide for yourself. I do know, that if we stand on what the word says, and wholeheartedly believe, we can achieve mighty miracles in all situations. For when we are weak and rebound it shows God's ultimate power. But it also has to do with our own attitude towards that situation. How we handle certain things can have a lot to do with the outcome of it. God is always there. But how do we react? Every person in this world has at one time, or another had a "thorn in their flesh" or a situation or conflict. But we have to remember, even though we go through these times of difficulty, we go through it, not stay in it. Keep in mind even if we are insulted, or go through hardships and are persecuted for our beliefs, that once and for all it was finalized by Jesus who conquered all of them on the cross. Meaning we must always 'believe' and never lose sight of 'faith' in our continued walk with Jesus. Only by 'faith,' truly 'believing,' and through 'grace' do we get through difficulties and calamities. His 'grace' is sufficient, for His 'power' is made 'perfect in our weaknesses.' We must always focus on God's love for us in our weaknesses. For in doing so we glorify our Lord. We may go through our life here on this earth with many troubles that come and go, but the ultimate experience of eternal life we will have is promised by Christ, with Christ.

Getting and being home was a mixed blessing. A blessing for I was home, but the combination of being exhausted, still not being able to eat fully, and being emotional where I would just start to cry for no reason was taking its toll. My husband would tell me, it was because of all of the anesthesia and medications that I was on while in the hospital. That it eventually would work its way out of my body and all would be well. As usual, he was right, but it did take time. I was so thankful to be in my own home with my precious husband and son, but the nights of no sleep was soon to come.

The surgeon would not sign off on a lift chair that I knew would be beneficial for me to sleep in. I couldn't lay flat. I knew that a recliner or lift chair would help in making me comfortable so I could sleep, for the next few weeks or even months. It would've been completely covered by our insurance company, but my surgeon was adamant that he 'would not sign off on such a thing.' The problem was we did not have a primary doctor at that time, so the surgeon also acted as my primary care doctor. Night after night my sweet husband would try to stack the pillows this way, and then we would try that way, trying to make me comfortable so I could get through the night. I would go from the couch, and then to a big chair trying to find relief, but becoming so exhausted and frustrated as the night progressed. Typically I would sleep for 2 hours and then wake up and stay awake for about 3 hours. Fall back to sleep for around 4 hours, then wake up again, exhausted to begin the day.

It also took a couple of weeks for me to master everyday tasks. When I first got home I had to use a walker everywhere I went in the house. I had to use it to push myself up off the couch. And taking a shower was a huge event, for I couldn't even stand in the shower, but had to sit while Jim stood outside making sure I was okay. Thank God we had a large walk-in shower in our master suite, for God provided that as well. Then one day I started to be able to do simple everyday tasks. I could lift my leg up to put socks on. The next day I could bend over and dry my legs as I got out of the shower. And the day after that I could even get up from the couch by just standing up. When that happened, I tried walking into the kitchen without the walker. I did it! Then I tried later to get up again and walk into the bathroom. I could do that as well. Everyday tasks started to come back one by one, and as they came, I mastered each one.

Another bright spot that happened in those first few weeks of being home was having in-home nursing care as well as a physical therapist that came to our house. Just like clockwork one or two days a week the nurse would come. Same with the PT that would come once a week. It was a blessing to have a nurse, come and check my vitals and track my progress. The PT that came out was extremely helpful. She gave me a set of 5 exercises that I was to do twice daily. Still being quite weak, I could hardly lift my legs to the side or lay on my back and lift my legs. But I was determined to gain my strength, and I was faithful in doing as she said. I started with just 10 reps 2 times a day. When she came back the following week, she was amazed at my progress and added 10 more to make it 20 times for each of the 5 exercises still twice a day. As each week passed both the nurse and the PT watched my progress in gaining my strength and getting back to being myself. More and more exercises were given to me even adding weights and eventually leg weights could be added. Both ladies were encouraging and always noticed and commented on my progress from week to week.

I am also happy to report the unending nights of no sleep also came to an end. One day, I was lying on the couch, and I felt as if God said: "Just go in and try to lie on the bed." I thought, "Well what I have to lose?" So I went into the bedroom, and I hopped right up on the bed and laid down. I couldn't believe it! I yelled, "Praise God!" I called out to my husband, "Jim come in here quick!" He rushed in, "Is something wrong?" He said with concern on his face. "No!

Look at me I'm on the bed I just hopped right up here" I said with excitement. "You are on the bed" he exclaimed with enthusiasm. I told him to get me another pillow to use with the pillows on the bed. I laid back with a sigh. It was a perfect sigh of contentment and relief. Later that night as I went to bed I said to myself, "sweet sleep." For it was the sweetest sleep I had in weeks. I knew that phrase was in the Bible for I had seen it. In the morning I woke up and I found it. It's in Proverbs 3:24, and it says, "When you lie down, you will not be afraid; Yes, you will lie down and your sleep will be sweet" (NKJV). I slept like a baby that first night in bed. I thanked God repeatedly for such a blessing and His grace. My sleep was 'sweet,' and I absolutely knew I had definitely turned a corner.

CHAPTER 13

THE MERRIEST OF CHRISTMASES

Before you knew it, the holidays were upon us. Christmas! My favorite time of year. I had been in the hospital the first week or so of December, and my husband and son took it upon themselves to "Deck the Halls" while I was gone. I remember coming home that first day and just giggling with delight as I looked at all the decorations and admired their work. I exclaimed, "I just love it! I wouldn't change a thing. You two did a great job," and they did. It was the week of Christmas and just a few days away that I had my first big outings.

At this time still being very frail, I would go out for only a short period of time before having to return home to rest. But I persevered, and with each outing, I became stronger and stronger. The first outing was to the salon with my dear friend Sally. Upon walking into the shop, it screamed "Merry Christmas." It was so delightful to see all the decorations complete with a little Christmas tree. There was a coffee table set with fresh baked cookies and fudge. I couldn't eat any, but it was wonderful for all of her clients to partake of.

My second outing was to the grocery store a day or two away from Christmas itself. My husband drove all three of us to the store. I remember stepping out to get into the car and the crisp cold air hitting my face. I took a deep breath, it was invigorating. We drove up to the store, and my son helped me out of the car. Freshly cut greens of garlands and wreaths were on display at the entrance in front of the store, and scent of pine smelled so good. The red kettle was out, and a cheery man rang a bell calling to all "Merry Christmas." We got a cart and began our shopping. I can't believe how many people we ran into that day that we knew. It was as if everybody was out picking up those last-minute items. Well wishes just poured in from each one followed by, "You look great!" I felt great! It was so special to do something as ordinary as grocery shop.

Before I knew it, Christmas Eve had come. I managed to make a little Christmas Eve dinner for my husband, son, and I. They certainly were a big help in preparing the turkey, mashed potatoes with gravy and of course the dressing. I couldn't disappoint my son by not making my famous dressing that he loves. We had a lovely dinner together and prepared for Santa to come that night.

The next morning we awoke to a light dusting of snow on the ground, and Santa had come. I was so happy that I had done most of my Christmas shopping in the fall of that year before everything happened in November. We relished opening our gifts and spending time together. Mostly the gifts were for our son, with family being out of state, but that's what makes it so much fun. Seeing the twinkle in his eye and the smile on his face with each gift that he opened.

Later that afternoon we went to Sally's house. It was such a pleasure to be with dear friends and celebrate Christmas Day together. I took a bottle of Ensure and my water bottle just in case I couldn't eat the delicious goodies that I knew she would have. Just spending time with people you care about is sometimes more than enough.

As we drove home later that evening, my heart was full of joy, and I felt so blessed. After my shower, I snuggled into a large fluffy throw on the couch. Christmas music was gently wafting through our home, and I watched the twinkling lights of the Christmas tree and the flickering of candles around the room. I thought to myself, "This, was the best Christmas ever." To be surrounded by people I love most including dear friends is a gift in itself. I was so thankful to God for all of His blessings toward my family, and my miracle of being alive and healed. For that was the greatest gift of all.

CHAPTER 14

WE GOT THIS

I can honestly say that my husband Jim and I became old pros at removing and attaching the colostomy bag. We absolutely had it down to a science. He even made a covering for the bag when I was in the shower. On nights that I was to change the bag every three to four days, I would go into the shower and just enjoy being able to soap up and rinse off, without being concerned about the bag. For if the bag got wet the adhesive would lift and it would start to come off.

Jim would prepare the fresh new bag as I removed the old one, thoroughly cleaning the area around the stoma. I would use a special wipe on any redness, then sprinkle the stoma powder on and dust it off. My skin would become red and even raw, but routine use of the wipe and powder helped immensely. I would then stretch the adapt barrier ring, made of natural rubber, placing it around the stoma itself. He would then hold the bag up to the area seeing where to place it through a 'peekaboo hole' in the bag. "Ready, aim, fire" he would say as he put the bag on. "Now off you go" he would finish with. "Aye aye, Captain" I would answer, and with the palm of my hand firmly holding the bag would go into the living room, settling into the couch, watch TV, keeping the warmth from my hand on the bag for 10 minutes as the adhesive would adhere to my skin.

As I now look back and reflect, there were a few moments that might not have been as funny at the time as they are now. Like the very first time I ever had a blowout! I never had one before, so I didn't know what to do. It was a major blowout. It had oozed out all over my side and was a mess. I was beside myself. But not Jim, solid and steady as always. "Don't worry you've got this" he said calmly, and I did. I went into the shower and rinsed around the bag then removed it cleaned the rest of the area, applied a fresh bag and everything was fine.

I can recall another time when we picked our son up from school and went to our midweek dinner out. We were just sitting having conversation, laughing and eating our meal when a small blowout happened. "Excuse me," I said, "I'll be right back." By this time I knew it was no big deal, so when I returned, I whispered in my husband's ear explaining what happened. He smiled. "We'll just go home after this. You don't mind do you, Jim?" He asked our son. "No I'm good with that" he replied. And that's exactly what we did no worse for the wear.

Looking back now, it wasn't that horrible to have a colostomy bag. After you got used to it, it almost becomes second nature. And if that was the only thing I had to bear for a short period of time, I could absolutely do that. God has shown me His 'grace,' and I could endure all things under that grace. From the very beginning, I had faith that God would not forsake me, nor that I would perish. I stood on that faith and will always stand on that faith. "For we walk by faith, not by sight"— 2 Corinthians 5:7 (NKJV).

For anyone going through a situation, there are many verses in the Bible about faith during difficult times. Here are a few:

- "And all things, whatsoever ye shall ask in prayer, believing, ye shall receive."— Matthew 21:22 (KJV)

- "But without faith it is impossible to please him: for he that cometh to God must believe that he is, and that he is a rewarder of them that diligently seek him" — Hebrews11:6 (KJV)

- "For with God nothing shall be impossible"—Luke1:37 (KJV)

- "For by grace are ye saved through faith; and not of yourselves: it is the gift of God: Not of works, lest any man should boast."— Ephesians 2:8-9 (KJV)

- "That your faith should not stand in the wisdom of men, but in the power of God." —1 Corinthians 2:5. (KJV)

These Scriptures are a constant reminder of how God is always with us regardless of what we are going through. When feeling discouraged and dismayed, that is the time when we should praise and worship God and seek His face through His word.

CHAPTER 15

LITTLE THINGS MEAN A LOT

As each passing day became weeks, I started to gain my strength while eventually getting my appetite back. I really didn't have one until after New Year's. I was so tired of the same old thing and hungry for something different. We decided to go to one of our favorite little Asian restaurants that we all love, especially my son.

Upon walking in, I looked over all the fresh and delectable items on display. "Yum," I said, everything smelled so delicious, and I decided on white rice with orange chicken adhering to my special diet. I would've loved those crispy fresh vegetables, but I couldn't eat a lot of raw foods at the time. I had to be on a very strict diet and avoid many foods I would normally eat while the colostomy was in place. I could only choose white rice not even brown, for it was not on the diet. Even so, it was delicious! I don't know if it was so delicious because I hadn't had food like that for so long, or if it was just because the food there is always so fresh and yummy. Nonetheless, it was great.

This was the beginning of many such outings where my appetite would be stimulated, and I would start to gain my strength and feel like myself again. This also led to going out to lunch with dear friends and a sense of normalcy in my life. The process of rebounding had begun! As I grew stronger, I was able to do more around the house again. I started to do the laundry, cooking meals, and light housework. It felt so good to do all of these things that we take for granted, that are a part of our everyday life.

Even my family went back to their regular routine. My son started to have friends come over again after school on Fridays. We started going places and doing things as a family on the weekend. Most importantly I was able to attend church on Sunday, seeing all of those dear people that stood by us and with us, during those critical days. I felt as if I had crossed another milestone. It makes me think of Romans 8:37 "Yet in all these things we are more than conquerors through Him who loved us" (NKJV). I was a conqueror, for I had conquered some of the darkest days I had ever been through in my life. Each and every day I was able to conquer step by step while becoming myself again. Being back to where I was, and even better than where I was. And I know this was all through Christ Jesus who loves me.

With each milestone I crossed, it would cause me to pause and reflect on how I delight in the Lord. "Delight yourself also in the LORD and He shall give you the desires of your heart."- Psalms 37:4 (NKJV). I feel so blessed that I have the 'desires of my heart' with my precious husband and son. And now, even more, do I 'delight in the Lord' for the continued hope of health and happiness until He comes to take all three of us 'with a shout!' 1 Thessalonians 4:16 (NKJV). Maranatha!

CHAPTER 16

ALMOST THERE

The day finally arrived in February when I was to go to the surgeon and see when he could schedule my reversal. I was so excited as we walked into the surgeon's office. I was full of joy with anticipation. When the surgeon saw me, he couldn't believe how well I looked. He praised me for how far I had come. "Believe me it's not me, I thank God for this," I said, he smiled and nodded. He said to me, "I've never seen you like this before, but then again I met you at your lowest point." He was amazed at how much vitality I had because for the first time he could actually see my personality, and who I really was. But always being so cautious and airing on caution he said, "Before we make the final connection, I want you to have a colonoscopy. I just want to make sure everything is clean and good before we reattach." Looking back now I can see that this surgeon was extremely thorough and I'm so happy about it. The scheduling nurse checked the available dates, scheduled my appointment, and got me in right away. My visit with him was on a Friday, and my colonoscopy was scheduled for the following Wednesday.

I became nervous and more anxious as the date approached for the colonoscopy. It was because I knew a dear woman in Michigan that went in for a routine colonoscopy, got her intestine nicked by the surgeon, became septic, and died. But I can't be nervous, nor can I be anxious, for Philippians 4:6-8 is very clear on this issue, "Be anxious for nothing, but in everything by prayer and supplication, with thanksgiving, let your requests be made known to God; and the peace of God, which surpasses all understanding, will guard your hearts and minds through Christ Jesus" (NKJV). God already knew my request before I even asked. I just needed to enter His 'gates with thanksgiving,' 'praise Him' for what He was doing, and 'rest in His peace.' God makes it clear that He will guard our 'hearts' and 'minds' through Christ Jesus, but my mind at that time was not cooperating. Isn't that always where it starts? Have you noticed that Satan always comes against you with a thought in your mind? We always have to be aware of how and what is being said through our thoughts. Is it gentle and calm, even when you are prodded to do something? Or is it antagonizing and condemning, ridiculing you continually? Always know God comes as the first not as the latter. It is always to build you up and to teach you, never to beat you down and accuse you. As the Scripture says, "Resist the devil, and he shall flee." How true that is!

The preparation for my colonoscopy began that Sunday before I went in on the following Wednesday. We picked up the MiraLAX from the drugstore mixed it thoroughly, and let it set in the refrigerator for 2 days. On the day before the procedure, I could only have a morning meal. So I had a hardy breakfast at Cracker Barrel with my husband, Jim. It was absolutely yummy! We returned home, and around 3 o'clock that afternoon I began drinking the mixture. It wasn't that bad. The MiraLAX came with a little packet of lemon flavoring that you could add making it much easier to go down. I really think it's all about our attitude and how we react causing a situation to be easy or hard. The word of God speaks on this issue in Romans 12:12: "rejoicing in hope, patient in tribulation, continuing steadfastly in prayer" (NKJV). You can choose to have a 'good attitude' or a 'bad attitude.' It's your choice. God will always be there regardless, but it helps to be positive with a good attitude.

It was now February, and The Winter Olympics were ongoing. I watched figure skating on TV that night, which is one of my favorite events. It certainly helped to keep my mind off of drinking 64 ounces of the mixture. I tried drinking at least 4 to 5 glasses in the first hour, and I succeeded. "Well, halfway done," I said with glee. I then rested for an hour as per instructions. My stomach was absolutely full, and I was waiting with bated breath to start to alleviate all that water. Well, you get what you wish for. All of a sudden my colostomy bag started filling up like a balloon. "Wow," I said, and promptly got up and went straight to the bathroom. The next hour had begun, and I did the same thing again, and drank till all was gone, resulting in the same effect. Watching the lovely skaters and enjoying the artistry of each one made the time go by much quicker, and finally the last of the mixture had gone through.

The last thing I needed to do that night, was to take a shower using a special surgical soap that the hospital sent home with me after my pre-op appointment. With the day behind me, I finally was ready for bed. I went to bed that evening thanking God as I always do, and making sure if I had sinned against Him in any way, or did anything displeasing to Him that I would be forgiven. This is something I do every night. I slept exceptionally well that night. As the new day dawned I knew I was closer to the end of the tunnel, but this time I could actually see the light.

We left very early on Wednesday for my colonoscopy, and my dear friend Sally was right there to help us out again. She would come and take Jim to school later that day because we left before it was time for him to leave.

We arrived in Springfield, found a parking spot, and enter the hospital. We proceeded to the outpatient registry and signed in. Right on schedule, they took me back, and I started to prepare for the colonoscopy. The nurse came in for the usual checklist prior to any surgery. I always laugh when people are so amazed when they ask what pharmaceuticals I'm taking. I know most people my age are on a slew of medications. The nurse asked that day as they always do and I answered "A low dose beta blocker. I take half of it." "Wow," she said, "That's pretty good." I just smiled, laughed, and again thanked God. I had been on a beta blocker since my initial surgery when I was severely ill, and my blood pressure was crazy, and my heart rate was slightly elevated. I had hoped after all was said and done I could finally get off it. This would eventually happen after my reversal during the last appointment with the cardiologist. Again I say, But God!

After the initial check-in, and all vitals charted Jim, and I just sat back and relaxed for the designated time for the procedure. While we waited, he started sending out texts to all that we were in the hospital, and I was ready to go. Such sweet words began to flow in from each and every text received. Words of endurance, and encouragement, true prayers of faith. The nurse soon came in and started my IV. She gave me meds to relax, and before you I knew it, off I went with a kiss from my sweetheart.

The colonoscopy went extremely well. Not only did the surgeon check my colon, but he also checked the stoma to make sure that all was well there. After the procedure, the surgeon came out to speak to Jim and said, "Everything looks great. It's time to button this thing up, and schedule that reversal as soon as possible." That was music to Jim's ears, and when he told me it was music to mine too.

The next thing I knew I was in recovery and pretty much wide-awake. After the procedure, the nurse put just a temporary gauze over the stoma. Jim being prepared as always had brought a fresh bag for us to apply after the surgery. The nurses were quite impressed. They comment "Wow that is awesome that you brought everything with you." It was a good thing too. The colostomy bag that I was using was a different make than the ones they had on hand in the surgical room.

I got dressed, and we were ready to go. After being discharged, we were on our way. We stopped on our way home for a quick bite, then to pick up our son, and at last home. When we got home, I went into the house and sighed a big sigh, for I knew I was one more step closer to the end of this journey.

With everything clean as a whistle and ready to go, the day had come to set the date of my reversal surgery. The nurse called from the surgical group and told me the date and time for my surgery. I was thrilled! That was the exact day and time I was hoping for. I thought to myself, "If I could have a couple of days that we could do something fun with our son, then maybe I could get his best friends mom to pick him up and stay with them on the day of my surgery." The week of my surgery just so happens to fall on the same week of his spring break from school. I was hoping to plan some fun things for him to do before and during the time I would be in the hospital. I called the mom of his friend immediately to see if she could have Jim come over on the day of my surgery. She texted back a couple of days later and said, "We're going to be out camping Monday-Thursday, but I talked it over with my husband, and we would love to take Jim with us. He's a really good kid." I couldn't believe it! What a blessing and answer to prayer! Not only could Jim spend time with his best friend, but he could have a wonderful little vacation at the time of his spring break. I texted back immediately saying, "How kind and thoughtful their invitation was and that he would love to join them on their trip." Now that I knew Jim was taken care of for that week, I had one more project to tend to before I went in for surgery.

Can you believe I was called for jury duty? I got the letter in the mail two weeks prior to my surgery date and just started to laugh. Of all times to get jury duty! The funny thing is, I actually found out at that time I was in a pool of jurors starting in December 2017 and ending March 2018. I never even knew I was in a pool because I never got notified. The date that I was to appear as a juror was the exact same week I was going to be in the hospital for my surgery. I called the circuit court office and told the clerk I was to have surgery that same week. She told me I needed to get a letter from my doctor so I could be excused. I called the surgeons office and spoke to the secretary. She said as she laughed, "Boy talk about bad timing." I laughed and agreed, "You can say that again." We were headed up to Springfield in the next few days, so I told her we would pick up the letter then. We got the letter Friday, and I faxed it to the courthouse first thing Monday morning. The clerk accepted the excuse, and I was ready to focus on my final surgery.

The weekend before my surgery was especially busy. My son was invited to a birthday party, and I was busily packing for his campout starting on Monday. It just so happened that St. Patrick's Day fell on that same weekend. My family and I always go out and have a real St. Patty's Day meal consisting of corned beef and cabbage. I threw caution to the wind that day and had my corned beef and cabbage. I knew it would be stinky passing through the stoma, but it was delicious, and I enjoyed every bite, smelly and all. It's always so much fun to be together and keep our traditions.

On Sunday we went to church. The prayers that were sent up to the throne room on my behalf were precious. So many family and friends went to the throne during that time on my behalf. It was those dear people and their prayers, be it by text, phone, or in person that made such an impact. For there is 'power' in prayer, and I so appreciate it. A few days before my surgery, I had so many dear friends encouraging me and giving me a 'word.' Words like the surgery will be 'painless,' it will go 'quickly,' and 'the doctors will be amazed.' All of those prayers and words did come to pass, and I am so thankful and grateful to God. Yes, it was a very busy weekend prior to that great day I had been anticipating for months. It was very busy, but it was wonderfully busy. For all three of us, my husband, my son and I were together. And for all of us being together as a family is priceless! God's plan and His blessings ahead were definitely at work for all of us. Glory be to God!

CHAPTER 17

LIGHT AT THE END OF THE TUNNEL

Monday approached and the new week dawned before us. Our son was packed up and ready to go on his grand adventure with some wonderful people. Easter was just a few weeks away, and I took the opportunity to make sure I got my son Jim something special for his Easter basket. I had to do this before I went into the hospital. It was a perfect time because he was gone and had no idea what I was up to. I wanted to surprise him. The following day was Tuesday, and that meant that the whole process of cleaning out my intestinal tract would begin as before.

I started the day off with my husband Jim having a delicious breakfast in the morning at Cracker Barrel just as we did before. After my delicious breakfast, all food would stop at 12 noon. Then around 3 o'clock in the afternoon the whole process of cleansing would begin. I started to really have this down pat. I had just done this same process a month before when I went in for a colonoscopy.

The mixture had set in the fridge for 2 days, and it was time to start drinking. We again added the lemon flavoring that helped to get the mix down. This time I needed to do it not for a colonoscopy but to cleanse my intestinal tract especially at the stoma site for the final connection for my colostomy reversal. That night, I scrubbed down with the surgical soap which I would repeat upon waking first thing in the morning before leaving to go to the hospital. The night came and went so quickly, and I was ready to be on my way.

We left early in the morning and arrived at Cox South in Springfield. We really started to know our way around that hospital. I don't know if that's a good thing or not; nevertheless, we knew right where to go. We went to surgical sign in, and I was ready to be admitted. As I sat waiting to go in, I observed the people that were around me. They were there for some sort of surgical procedure, and we were all in the same boat. The look on their faces told where they were emotionally. You could see fear in their eyes, some just in a quandary, and I prayed silently, "Lord I hope they know or will find Jesus for I can't imagine going through something like this without Him."

Just as before, it didn't take long, and we were brought back to a room. While we waited Jim sent out texts to all to let them know I was there and ready to go. I ended up going into surgery about three hours after my scheduled time, with the operation itself taking about two hours and forty-five minutes to complete.

After recovery, I didn't get into a room until about 6 o'clock that evening. I woke up and there was my Jim. I didn't feel horrible, and I was pretty awake for just coming out of the anesthesia. We held hands and just chatted. He stayed until visiting hours were over and would return first thing in the morning. Surprisingly so, I slept quite well that night. I was told I had a pain pump that I could press if needed. I ended up not pushing that pain pump at all that first night. I actually ended up not using it except for one time; when they tightened my stitches at the stoma site. It wasn't that painful, but I remembered words spoken directly in prayer that there would be 'no pain,' and God answers prayer.

First thing in the morning, I felt refreshed and ready to start my recovery, so without wasting any time I got up and took a walk. I knew I needed to get moving as soon as possible. I started the day by doing 2 laps around the hospital hallway using a walker. Now again, this was no easy task for it was quite cumbersome. Not only did I have to use a walker, but I had a nurse beside me, pushing an IV pole that had a saline solution for the nutrients I needed, and a urine bag for I still had a catheter and a nose tube inserted, during that first walk. I took my first lap that morning and the second one later in the afternoon.

As I walked that morning, I saw my surgeon at one of the nurses' stations. I called out to him he looked up and gave me the biggest smile, "Hi! I'll be right in" he called back. "Okay, see you soon" I answered. Upon finishing my first lap, I met him back in my room. I could tell he was very pleased with seeing me up and about so early that morning. He said he would not be in the hospital over the weekend but would have one of the surgeons from his surgical group attending me. I was fine with that. I knew he would keep a watchful eye on me regardless of where he would be.

On that same day, I had the kindest nurse who was Ukrainian. I knew she was Ukrainian because I could detect her accent that was the same as my grandmothers, who was also from Ukraine. That nurse was encouraging and very attentive. She had a wonderful aide that assisted her and helped with the removal of the catheter, and then by giving me a sponge bath that morning which was awesome. Later that afternoon as we walked I told her my grandmother was from Ukraine. "Really," she said, and we proceeded to chat about my wonderful childhood memories of pierogies and borscht and of all the goodies my grandmother used to make. We giggled how it would literally take hours for her to prepare this wonderful food by making the dough, mixing all of the ingredients, and cooking everything together and how my sister, my mom and dad, and I would inhale every last morsel in just minutes.

It's remarkable how God puts people in your path. I'm always amazed by divine appointments and how God uses specific encounters to bring people together creating a giant puzzle. Piece by piece, they come together. It is a giant puzzle, but I also call them God appointments. You know, you're at this place, at this time, and this person just happens to be at the same place at the same time. God appointments. I actually had several God appointments during my stay in the hospital this last time.

I remember a young man, very handsome, who was an aide. He came into our room at the end of his shift and told my roommate and me that the next day would be his last day at the hospital. "Oh," I said, "I bet you're going back to school." He stood gazing out the window and said: "Why yes I am." I then asked, "What are you studying? He turned and looked at me smiling with a twinkle in his eye and said, "The ministry." "Oh, how exciting" I exclaimed. He then flashed that big smile again and said as he was leaving the room, "Well I better get going. I gotta finish up with my other patients."

At that moment I wished I could've talked to him about certain ministries that have programs for young people wanting to go into the ministry. I hoped he would find the right one. Well, guess what? The very next day he stopped in to say goodbye one last time. I seized the moment. I said, "Hey, have you ever heard of Perry Stone? He has a wonderful new online ministry school." "Humm..., Perry Stone...? No..., I don't think I ever have heard of Perry Stone. I'll check him out. I can remember Perry Stone. Thanks a lot "he said flashing that smile. "Do check it out! I think it might work for you" I smiled back, and off he went. I pray that young man finds his calling and completes his destiny that God has for him. It's so wonderful to see young people with the desire to serve God. It is so needed today. They need to be the spokesman for their generation, for time is short.

God also arranged that I could see the Ukrainian nurse one last time. I was up walking and met her in the hallway. I called out her name, and she said with her Ukrainian accent, "Oh... and look at you walking all by yourself." We hugged. I said, "Yes, and I'm going home today, Slava Bohu!" That means 'Praise God' or 'Glory to God' in Ukrainian. I hadn't said that in years and it came out perfect. She looked at me, then around, kind of giggled, smiled, and said very softly, "Yes, Slava Bohu." That phrase seemed to strike a chord in her from the distant past. She wasn't sure if she should say it out loud, but I'm glad she did. I don't know what her relationship is with the Lord, but I can pray and believe that she will have a genuine relationship with the Lord Jesus Christ, for now, is the time. It only takes one moment.

The tiniest seed in the world comes from the tropical orchid. That beautiful fragrant flower comes from one tiny seed that weighs just 10 billionths of an ounce, but when planted and nurtured will produce the most beautiful aromatic flower. It takes a little tiny seed, like an orchid seed, to be planted by just one word or some act of kindness, to ultimately change a person's life forever. We don't know at the time if it was planted in fertile ground and then rooted, but we have 'faith,' and faith is invisible. It isn't by sight, but by believing. Faith and believing is rock solid without a doubt, and where we take our stand on the 'truth.' "So then faith comes by hearing, and hearing by the word of God" -Romans 10:17 (NKJV).

We are to continually put out little seeds in all that we do and say, everywhere we go, and in all situations and events that come our way. For we never know where a person is, but God always knows. And that little tiny seed might be all they need to pursue a life with the Lord and fulfill their true destiny as they journey on this earth. What a lovely fragrant bouquet of flowers that each one of us can present to our Lord.

CHAPTER 18

PRAISE GOD FOR TOTAL RESTORATION

This time in the hospital was entirely different from the first time I was in the hospital. I always refer back to, I never really knew how sick I was, but praise God this time it was 180° turnaround. My surgeon came in the next morning after surgery and was delighted with my progress. He told me he would be out of the hospital Friday, Saturday, and Sunday, but another surgeon from their surgical group would be coming in each day to check on me. I knew my surgeon would keep a close eye on me no matter where he would be. He actually would be attending a Missouri Surgeons Conference that weekend. With that being said, I knew he would watch over me via the computer and know exactly what was happening.

    When he returned that following Monday, he said, "Oh I was keeping an eye on you. I knew everything that was going on." I smiled and kind of giggled and said, "I knew you were." He left knowing I was in good hands and that he would keep a watchful eye.

    On the second day, his colleague was there bright and early. He was standing by my bedside at 5:30 a.m. The bandaging on my incisions had some oozing coming out, and there was a little dried blood on my gown and on the top sheet of the bed. He unwrapped the bandaging and looked at the incisions. "Well, this looks great. Fine job" he said, and that's when he told me I might want to push the pain pump for he was going to tighten the sutures where the stoma was. The site of the stoma wasn't completely sutured. This was purposely done, for my surgeon wanted it to continue to drain to make sure all the waste was out and completely clean. The surgeon proceeded to pull out all the packing including the gauze down deep in the stoma itself, then pulled a few of the sutures together. He was right, it had quite a bite as he pulled those sutures tighter. He finished up and said, "I'll see you tomorrow morning. You're doing great."

The next day came. I couldn't believe it was already the third day after surgery. The surgeon was there bright and early as promised by 6:00 a.m. "I bet you want that thing out of your nose," he said, referring to the tube that went through my nose, past my throat, and down into my stomach. "Oh, boy do I ever," I said with a sigh. "Well, I'll tell you what, I'll start you on clear liquids. If you don't have a problem I'll take it out first thing tomorrow morning" he added. "Great" I answered with relief.

That was the first day since the day before my surgery that I had anything in my stomach. I didn't even have water up to that point, let alone clear liquids. He put the order in, and by that morning I had a clear liquid breakfast. I took it really easy. I started by slowly sipping some apple juice. It tasted like fresh apples from the orchard. I sipped very carefully. Then I tasted a little bit of Jell-O. That was good too. Later for lunch, I had clear chicken broth. I was sitting up in bed drinking and enjoying my chicken broth, then all of a sudden I started to cough and gag. It was that tube! Even though my tummy said, "Yes please, more broth," the tube made it so difficult to drink. I decided I would stop for the day even though I was still very hungry. My stomach tolerated everything I ate, but it was very difficult to swallow with the tube down my throat.

Finally, it was the fourth day. And being true to his word the surgeon was there around 6 a.m. "You ready to get that thing out," he said referring to the tube, I nodded my head "Okay let's do it." He went over to the sink to wash his hands, put on gloves, and then came back to my bedside. As smooth as silk and without missing a beat he pulled 1, 2, 3 and that nose tube was out. WOW! What a relief it was! It was a quick and easy out, and I instantly felt great. I looked back at the two canisters behind me, and what had come out of my stomach. There was one canister completely full with a dark green liquid and another half full with a pale-yellow liquid. I asked the nurse about it, and he said, "That's all the bile that was in your stomach."

I had that nose tube before. It initially was when I first was admitted to the hospital. I had it while I was sedated and pretty much out, and only remember a couple of days of being awake and having it in the ICU before they removed it. The medical term used is a nasogastric tube or NG tube. Even though it is incredibly uncomfortable, it is so important to have after surgery. Bile is a bitter greenish alkaline fluid that aids digestion and is secreted by the liver and stored in the gallbladder. My poor roommate did not have the tube beginning in the nose and ending in the stomach. She had horrible nausea and was so uncomfortable. Even though it's not the most pleasant experience, I am very thankful my surgeon always takes the precaution to insert the tube during surgery to get rid of all excess bile in the stomach.

The acting surgeon then said, "Now for today I'm going to start you on solid liquids and see how that goes." "Yes," I said, as I shook my head. He didn't waste a minute and made sure I got a solid liquid breakfast that morning. I had my apple juice and cream of wheat. It was heaven! No more tube, and no more saline. He stopped the saline solution through the IV that morning as well. Thank God, I was finally being untethered! In the afternoon I had creamy potato soup and creamy tomato soup for the evening meal. The soups were always accompanied by either Jell-O or pudding and either iced tea or juice.

The nurses would come in and out throughout the day checking and tending to my roommate and me. They always would ask the same thing "Any rumblings? Are you passing gas yet?" "No, not yet" we would answer with a sigh. To pass the time and the evening my roommate and I watched a wonderful Hallmark movie. She fell asleep, and as soon as it was over, I turned the TV off. I couldn't really get to sleep that night. All I kept thinking about was, "Boy, I hope I pass gas soon." I relaxed, and I started to pray and thought of all the blessings that God had given me and my family. I then heard God saying very clearly in my mind, "You know I've got this, close your eyes and pray in the Spirit for other people." "Oh yes Lord of course" I whispered. I did as the Lord said and shut my eyes and one by one the faces of all different people came before me. I did as the Lord said and started praying in the Spirit for each person as they melted one into another. They weren't related to one another, but I kept praying as each face came to mind. I thought, "Oh Lord how selfish am I to not think of all these people that are going through situations themselves and think only of myself."

Suddenly, around 11:30 p.m. I felt rumblings in my tummy. Then, like a trumpet announcing a grand event, it sounded, and gas came out! I started to giggle with such joy. I had conquered the first hurdle. My bowels were finally waking up! Later that same night I passed even more gas. I thought back on praying for people and how important it is. Sometimes we have to take our eyes off ourselves so God can work, not only in our lives but in others. And as with all things of life, we find this too in the word of God.

- "Praying always with all prayer and supplication in the Spirit, and watching thereunto with all perseverance and supplication for all saints;"—Ephesians 6:18 (KJV)

- "Now I beseech you, brethren, for the Lord Jesus Christ's sake, and for the love of the Spirit, that ye strive together with me in [your] prayers to God for me;" — Romans15:30 (KJV)

I had such incredible peace and the sweetest sleep that night. For soon and soon I knew all of this would be behind me, and before long, I drifted off to dreamland.

The next morning, I woke up refreshed and excited. I decided to go on my daily walk first thing that morning before having breakfast. Now, I had walked faithfully every day from the first day of my recuperation. The day after surgery, I walked 2 laps using a walker, still having the nose tube inserted, being connected to an IV pole, accompanied by a nurse, who also assisted with a urine drainage bag for I still had the catheter inserted. The first day was the hardest with all of that paraphernalia I had to drag with me, but I did it. On the second day I took 4 laps still connected to an IV pole, assisted by a nurse, with the nose tube still in place, but thank goodness the catheter had been removed. The third day I went for 6 laps with only an IV pole, walking on my own, accompanied by a nurse and sometimes not. But today, Sunday, I would take 8 laps around the hospital hallway all by myself free of all medical equipment that had been attached to me. It felt so good to walk, and that I had taken such great strides in accomplishing something each and every day.

I was still on a soft liquid diet, but then something wonderful happened in the afternoon. I came back from one of my walks on that Sunday afternoon and felt the urge to have a bowel movement. I went to the bathroom and to my delight it finally happened, I had my first bowel movement! It was so natural as if I had never even had surgery. I was giddy! I couldn't wait to tell the nurse. I pushed the call button, and the nurse came right in. "I've got great news! I had my first bowel movement," I said with a big smile. The nurse was so excited she started clapping her hands then saying, "Well I can see you'll be going home soon." Jim came to the hospital about an hour later. I couldn't wait to tell him. He too was so excited and happy that all was going well, and we both knew I would be going home soon.

CHAPTER 19

HOME FROM A LONG JOURNEY

It was Monday morning, and my surgeon was finally coming back after his weekend conference. I was so excited, I knew I had done exceptionally well with my walking and all I was to do. I had met all the criteria that were required of me to be discharged so that I could go home. He came in and gave me that big smile. "Well you are doing really great," he said, "I can't see any reason to keep you here." I exclaimed, "I can really go home?" "I'll tell you what he said, we'll have you eat a solid lunch. If you don't have any problems, you can go home this afternoon." I was delighted!

Usually, all of our meals were served right on time, and lunch would arrive around 11 a.m. But on that particular day lunch was served late. Of course, it was late that day. I was hoping it would be early because the sooner it was there the sooner I could go home. I can recall being so hungry for real food that no matter what they gave me it would've tasted good. It actually was pretty good. I had a chicken breast with wild rice pilaf and carrots. They even gave me a piece of chocolate cake with chocolate frosting for dessert. My stomach had shrunk again, so I could only eat about half of it, but I enjoyed every bit of it. I had no issues and I even had a large bowel movement before I left the hospital.

My roommate's surgeon came in one morning a few days earlier and had made a bet on which one of us would be discharged first. "Now the first one who gets discharged gets this," he said, as he waved a dollar bill in the air before taping it to the wall. We laughed as he did that. It looked like I would be the first to leave, but not really, for we were really going home at the same time. I said to her "How about we rip the dollar in half since we're really being discharged at the same time." "No, you're really leaving first. What's fair is fair," She answered. "Are you sure? If we ripped it in half, we could each have a keepsake" I laughingly said. "No you keep it" she answered. "Okay" I said.

Jim had gone to the nurses' station to tell them I had no problems with my solid lunch and they answered "We'll be right in with the paperwork." He brought some of my clothes from home, and I was happily putting them on preparing to leave. The paperwork soon arrived. We signed everything, and we were ready to go. Jim went to get the car and the nurse came with a wheelchair to assist me through the hallway one last time.

As we went down the hallway, I thought, "How ironic that this journey began on this very floor with my abdomen being open for five days and now ending with my colostomy reversal and recuperation from surgery on that same floor." We chatted as we went through the main lobby to the front doors. Soon Jim was there with our Jeep. I didn't even need that much assistance to get in.

As we drove away, I looked out on the hustle and bustle of Springfield. It felt so good to see all the people and busyness of the day. A light rain started to fall as we made our way onto the highway. As we got closer to our home, I reflected on those last few days in the hospital and thought, "Thank God I'm almost home. I'm going home. Home!" As we turned onto the winding road that leads to our home a great joy filled my heart, and I was content. This long journey had finally come to an end. But the miracle I experienced of what God had done for me would never end.

This time being home and recuperating from surgery was a breeze and utterly different from the first surgery. I came home and felt so good that I had to be careful not to overdo it. I had to keep reminding myself, "Just take it easy. You have internal stitches and sutures and staples on the outside." I wasn't to lift anything heavy, that being anything over 5lbs, and was limited to specific activities around the house. I wasn't able to drive, so I had plenty of time to concentrate on finishing this book. I had so much energy and felt amazingly good. This time sleep was a piece of cake. I jumped right up on the bed that first night home and had the sweetest sleep ever.

One week after being home I had my first postoperative or post-op appointment with my surgeon. We drove to Springfield the Monday after Easter so the surgeon could check on how all was going. He was extremely pleased and told me "You know, it's pretty amazing that you were out of the hospital in 4 short days after such a major surgery. You were discharged early afternoon on the 5th day." I shook my head yes, thinking, "Only God could do that." A phrase kept running through my mind over and over. It was "The doctors would be amazed," and he used the word 'amazed.' Those words were given to me by several people just days before my final surgery. "I'm a miracle," I said with conviction. He finished our conversation by saying, "Next week I'll remove your staples. Everything's looking great. See you next week." "Okay," I answered. Jim and I left his office, and I stood in awe for what God had done.

One week to the day, we went back, and my staples were removed. What a relief it was! Just getting the staples out felt so good for I could now move again and didn't have all of those tiny staples poking continually in my stomach.

My next post-op visit would be with the cardiologist. I chose to see the nurse practitioner to get the date that was most convenient for us. He works very closely with the cardiologist and is on the exact same page. He was the same one that I saw in the hospital when I was initially given the beta blocker. I was thrilled when I walked in and the nurse saw me and declared, "You look fabulous!" "I feel fabulous" I answered. My blood pressure was 123/70, my heart rate was in the high 60s, with an oxygen level at 98. They actually gave me a choice to continue on that little half of a beta blocker or not. "I would love to get off of it," I said with delight. "Do I have to do something special to get off of it?" I questioned. "No. You can just stop taking it tomorrow" he answered. "Now if you do have any problems such as heart palpitations or shortness of breath contact us immediately" he added. I then inquired "Will I know right away?" He answered, "Not necessarily. So I want to make sure you know how to take your pulse." He proceeded to show me how to take my pulse with two fingers on my wrist. I found it right away, and it was quite easy.

Getting off that beta blocker was huge for me. That was the last medication that I was on, and now it was gone. Praise God! The practitioner said, "You may have been on this because at the time you were so weak, and you did have issues with your blood pressure and heart rate in the beginning. I'm believing that it was just temporary, and you won't have to ever be on it again." "I absolutely agree," I said confidently. After that day, I knew each step I took with each post-op appointment was placed perfectly by the hand of God.

My last post-op appointment with my surgeon was very special. Not only did I find out that it wasn't 6 inches of my large intestine that was removed, but almost 12 inches or 1 foot of my intestine. He explained after all the diseased tissue had been removed that the additional intestine was specifically related to where the stoma site was and where the reversal occurred. He had removed all of the diseased tissue and then some from the stoma site making sure it was now just part of my intestine. This made it not 6 inches, but almost 1 foot. He also removed all of the old scar tissue during the second and final surgery. As always airing on caution my surgeon said: "You can come back in a month if you feel you need to." I just laughed and said to my husband, "He just wants to see me," and we all laughed. My surgeon said, "Just call if you need to come in or if anything comes up." I thanked him for all he had done, and he graciously posed with me as my husband took a picture of the two of us.

After leaving his office, I said to Jim, "I really want to go back to the ICU to see it and hopefully see some of the nurses that I had." He said "Okay let's go," and we did. It was a very odd feeling walking into the ICU wing of the hospital. Jim really knew his way around for he had taken this trek many a time before. As we walked, I just looked around trying to jar my memory and recall events in certain locations, and it did. We came to the room that I had been a patient in for so many weeks, and it looked so small. I just stood there and looked inside it seemed so surreal. The kitchenette looked slightly different than I remembered and the nurses' station was right there just as I recalled. We started to tell the nurse on duty that I had been a patient in that room back in November. She was amazed by hearing my story an seeing me now.

As we stood chatting with her a group of nurses passed by and Jim said, "There's that one nurse! Come on let's catch up to her." We caught up to her, and Jim got her attention. She took one look at us, and her mouth dropped open. She couldn't believe her eyes and said, "Oh my goodness! How are you?" Then turning to me continued to say, "You look so wonderful absolutely beautiful!" I laughed, and she proceeded to tell us other nurses that had been with me were on call at the hospital that day, and she wanted to go and find them. She returned and had a couple of nurses with her. They were so excited to see me as I am now, healthy and completely restored. They inquired if I had the reversal yet and then exclaimed, "That's fantastic!" The one nurse asked if they could take a picture together with me, for they wanted to put up pictures on one of the walls showing people that had successful recoveries saying "It encourages other patients and their families." I said, "Of course." We talked about how my mind was telling me one thing, but I was experiencing another. I asked them about a patient dying and a funeral service happening. One of the nurses said " Oh that type of thing happens very often especially if the person is from out of town and the family wants something done right away. It helps with comforting the family during the time of their loss." I told them how I felt like I was being held prisoner and tied up. Then we laughed as I told them my husband would say how you would gently remind me, "Now Lisa don't pull those tubes out okay." And the nurses came back with, "But you'd try to pull those tubes out anyway," then roared with laughter because they knew I would try to do it again.

I giggled as I told them about this doctor that came in and would go to the Italian restaurant. Prompting one of the nurses to say "Oh you must have had doctor so-and-so. He and another doctor went to this Italian Café not far from the hospital all the time." "Really?" I said "Wow! Maybe I heard them talking subconsciously, but I kept thinking it was down the hall in the hospital and there was a statue of Mussolini outside of it." They just started to roar with laughter again. The one nurse asked about my son and how he was doing which touched me for she really remembered everything about my family.

Our visit came to an end with both nurses thanking me again and again for coming back to see them. I also thanked them for being so wonderful through my journey when I was so ill. They kept saying "We never really know what happens when people leave after being severely ill. It's wonderful to see when people are so vibrant and totally recovered." I said to them, "I know that it was nothing short of a miracle that got me through this illness and all that I went through." One of the nurses started to slowly nod her head saying, "I believe that." I then said, "I believe God's hand was totally in this." The two nurses standing there both nodded their heads, and one said "Absolutely! I totally agree with that." "Me too," said the other nurse and both were standing in agreement on this miraculous miracle by God's hand. This is tremendous in itself! These nurses saw situations like mine every day and knew the severity of it. Yet they acknowledged the miracle of me still being here 'by God' and 'God alone.' My visit to the ICU was so important because not only did I get to see these wonderful people so dedicated to their care for me, but it truly made my heart sing when the nurses, knew and acknowledged that I experienced a 'mighty miracle' that could only be done 'by the hand of God.' This is the cherry on top of the sundae. To God and God alone be the glory!

CHAPTER 20

TWO TRUTHS-A MIRACLE AND THE GUT

The purpose of this book is to highlight two absolute truths. First and foremost that God, Yahweh, is real and His Son Jesus Christ is seated at His right hand. From there He does mighty miracles each and every day. This isn't an opinion, this is a fact and the complete and utter truth. This is essential and must be unequivocally understood. All glory goes to God and to God alone for any and all actual miracles. The second truth is that God has created our bodies meticulously. We are very intricately made. Proving the gut to be one of the core disease fighting systems of the human body, and is central to our health, vitality, and well-being.

(Gut Brain Axis)[7]

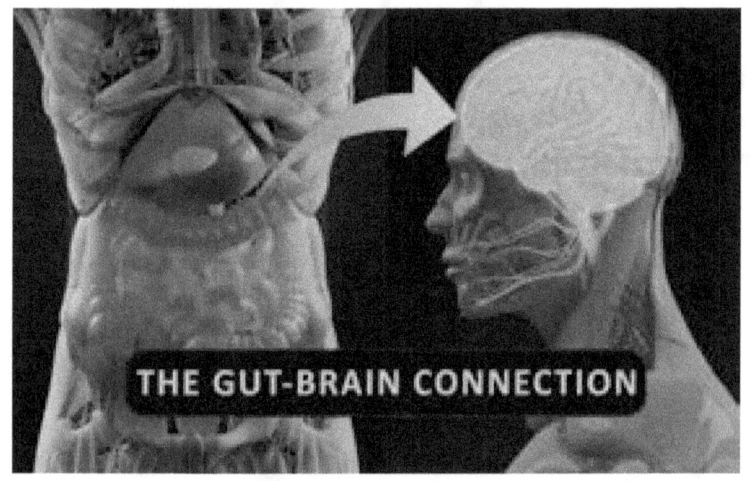

(Intestinal Microbiome)[8]

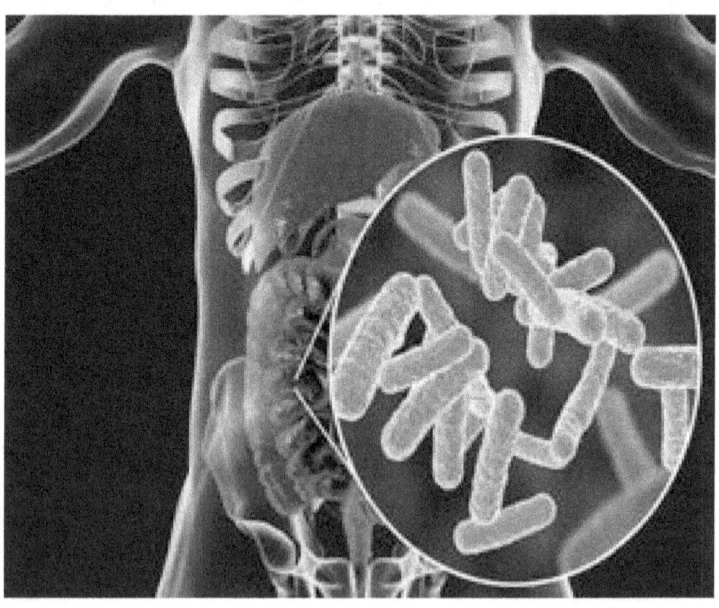

(Intestinal Flora)[9]

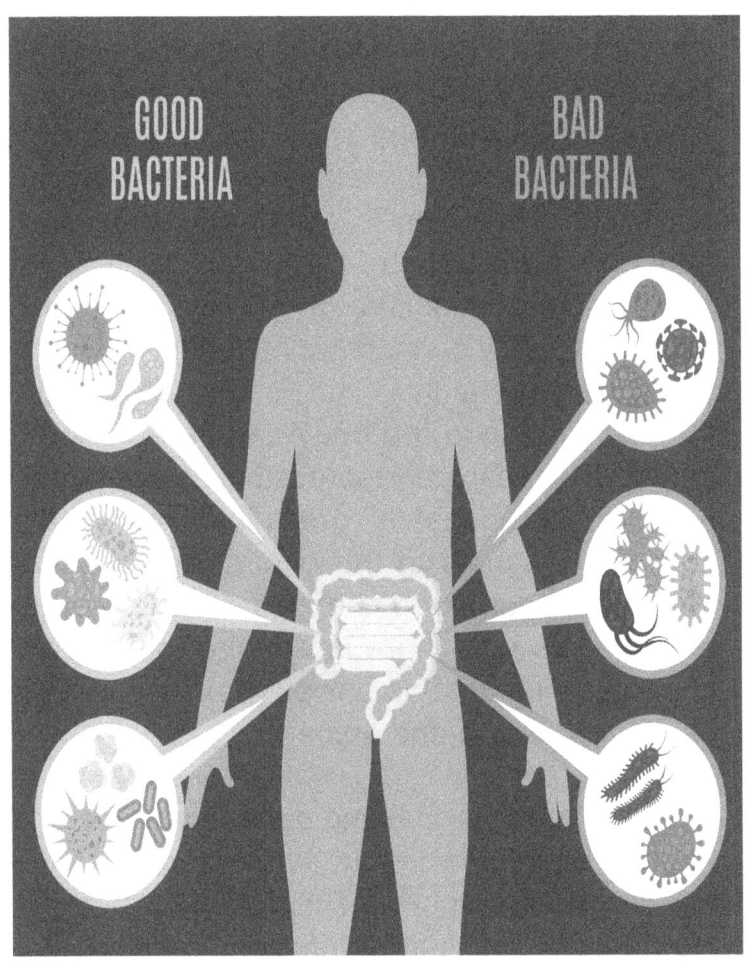

In recent discoveries, the gut now reveals that its importance is much more far-reaching than just aiding in digestion. It's also known as "the little brain" or "the second brain." Have you ever had a gut feeling? Have you ever felt butterflies in your stomach? If so, these feelings are very real and so is the connection to the "brain" in our gut, and the "main brain" in our skull. The brain in our head has a direct effect on the stomach, also known as the 'gut' and the gastrointestinal, or GI tract, with both being intimately connected, meaning they communicate constantly. This is why certain diseases can plague the body and be a very real cause of stress and depression. Science has now discovered that the gastrointestinal system may send signals to the central nervous system that trigger mood changes. These findings may explain why there is a higher percentage of people with irritable bowel syndrome that develop depression and anxiety.

There is research being done today that links the two brains and might even affect cognitive thinking and memory. This research is ongoing at John Hopkins Medical Center. It can also affect movement and contractions of the GI tract, making inflammation worse and your body more susceptible to infection. Many doctors today are linking inflammation itself as the root cause of both illness and disease. The GI tract in our gut, from end to end, starts in the esophagus and continues to the anus.

Digestive disorders are numerous and can range from irritable bowel syndrome or IBS to colitis, diverticulitis and Crohn's disease. Liver disease is also included for the vital role the liver has in the digestive process. Roughly 70% of your immune system is located in the digestive system. Serotonin is well known as a brain neurotransmitter. It is estimated that 90% of our body's serotonin is made in the digestive tract. This research comes from Caltech. You also have 10 times as many microbes as cells in your body. A microbe is a microscopic organism. In other words, 10 times more bacteria are living in your digestive tract, then there are cells in your entire body. Bad gut bacteria promotes inflammation and can impact your rational decision-making and can cause anxiety or depression. It may even influence which foods you like and dislike. You have 100 times more DNA in your microbiome then in all the cells of your entire body. The DNA in your cells and in your microbiome communicate with each other. Our gut also houses good bacteria, which protects us against infection and helps to run our metabolism. We must continually make an effort to keep harmful bacteria at bay and good bacteria levels up. The daily grind of the gut is essential to good health. It is responsible for breaking down food, absorbing the nutrients, and expelling the waste through muscle contractions moving everything through our system and out. With our diet, medications, and daily stress and anxiety, it's no wonder millions of Americans are affected each day with some type of gut issue.

As we begin to age, starting at 50, our good gut bacteria starts to decline causing our gut acidity to fall. This is why pathogens and yeast begin to attack our gut causing more illnesses as we age. A quote penned by the great Shakespearean writer reads, "To be, or not to be, that is the question." Therefore I pose the question, and question being, should our body be acidic or alkaline? The answer may surprise you for both are correct. PH is a measurement used to determine the level of acidity or alkaline in your body. A pH of 7 is water. Any number above that is alkaline; a number below acidic. Bile is an alkaline substance with a pH of 7-8, produced in the liver. The gallbladder stores the bile until it is needed to aid in digesting fatty foods.

Remember a few chapters before when I was in the hospital and had the nose tube? It went through my nose, past my throat, and down into my stomach. It was to remove all bile, a greenish fluid, in the stomach which was alkaline, thus making the gut acidic. Pathogens are bad bacteria and having acid in the gut kills the pathogens and keeps them in check. You need an acid gut, but you need alkaline cells in your organs and immune system for optimal health. This can be quite confusing to many, which doesn't surprise me, for people are taught you need to be alkaline and never acidic. Acidity in the gut fosters the growth of friendly bacteria which can provide a boost to the immune system. Your body should always be alkaline at a minimum level of about 7.32 -7.36. The cells of your body work best when they are alkaline, and this is made possible by having a diet of foods that are rich in potassium and magnesium. This can be achieved by adding such foods as spinach, almonds, and dark chocolate.

(Fermented Vegetables in Jar)[10]

(Fermented Food Sampler)[11]

(Jars with pickles, green tomatoes, cayenne pepper, mixed salad and chillies)[12]

(Organic Vegetables and Legumes)[13]

(Fermented Preserved Vegetables)[14]

Fermented foods also improve gut health. Fermentation is the process by which a substance breaks down into a simpler substance. Microorganisms like yeast and bacteria usually play a role in the fermentation process. When food is fermented, it's left to set and steep until the sugars and carbs become bacteria boosting agents. Common fermented foods you can add to your diet are sauerkraut, pickles, and kefir that tastes like drinkable yogurt. The consumption of fermented foods has many health benefits. The microflora that lives in fermented foods creates a protective lining in the intestines and shields it against Salmonella and E. coli. Fermented foods lead to an increase of antibodies and a stronger immune system that can regulate the appetite and reduce sugar and refined carb cravings. It is a known fact that fermented vegetables can help treat Candida or yeast in the gut.

We should make it a point to stay away from foods that are GMO or genetically modified food. These foods are man-made and questionable in the vital nutrients we need. Foods that are white in color tend to be processed and refined. By that, I mean foods that are white in color are high in starch and are simple carbs. These foods are white rice, white bread, white pasta, white potatoes, and simple sugars like table sugar and high fructose corn syrup.

These foods all strip away beneficial fibers and are converted to sugar which is stored in the body as fat.

With the awareness of this, should we always try to eat a healthy diet and be in prayer, without ceasing, for our total health and well-being daily? Of course, we should. Remember the saying, "let food be thy medicine and medicine be thy food." We are responsible for this body here on earth until God gives us our heavenly body. We should make sure that we feed our body the nutrients it needs by eating raw foods such as fresh fruit, particularly fresh raspberries, and strawberries. We can boost gut health by eating more pectin's which are found in apples, pears, and citrus fruits including the peel. Fresh vegetables consisting of carrots, peas, broccoli, and brussels sprouts. High protein and healthy fats from nuts and avocados should also be a part of a healthy gut diet. Whole grains such as barley and plenty of beans, whether they're black, kidney, pinto, or you name it, they are a glorious source of fiber.

Remember, God the Father initiated the rainbow, and we should try to eat the rainbow every day. In other words, foods that are rich in color are always more beneficial to our bodies, and our Heavenly Father only wants the best for His children. We see this in Genesis 9:3

"Every moving thing that liveth shall be meat for you; even as the green herb have I given you all things." (KJV) Also in Genesis 1:29 "And God said, Behold I have given you every herb bearing seed, which is upon the face of all the earth, and every tree, in the which is the fruit of a tree yielding seed; to you it shall be for meat." (KJV) And finally, 1 Corinthians 10:31 (KJV) "Whether therefore ye eat, or drink, or whatsoever ye do, do all to the glory of God." God makes it very clear that we are to nourish and feed our body and to do it onto the Glory of God.

What is alarming to me is the number of brothers and sisters in Christ that are being afflicted with some disorder of the gut. I mean, brothers and sisters that are committed believers in Jesus Christ and stand on the word of God. It made me think there's more to it than just diet, medications and so on. It prompted me to see what does the Bible actually has to say about our body and particularly the gut. The prophet Hosea writes in chapter 4:6 "My people are destroyed for lack of knowledge..." I believe this knowledge covers all areas of our life, spiritually, mentally, physically, and emotionally. He finishes the Scripture by saying, "...Because you have rejected knowledge, I also will reject you from being priest for Me; Because you have forgotten the law of your God I also will forget your children." (NKJV) It is vital that we seek out Godly wisdom and knowledge in all aspects of our life using the word of God.

Different categories in the Bible deal directly with the stomach. Let's take a look at some of the Scriptures that refer to the stomach or gut:

1. Afflictions of the stomach:

- "Drink no longer water, but use a little wine for thy stomach's sake and thine often infirmities."— 1 Timothy 5: 23 (KJV)

2. The stomach and God's judgment and a symbol of worldliness:

- "Whose end is destruction, whose God is their belly, and whose glory is in their shame- who set their mind on earthly things."—Philippians 3:19 (NKJV)

3. Crawling on ones stomach as a sign of submission:

- "They shall lick the dust like a serpent, they shall move out of their holes like worms of the earth: they shall be afraid of the Lord our God, and shall fear because of thee."— Micah 7:17 (KJV)

4. An empty stomach, as a warning:

- "The righteous eats to the satisfying of his soul, but the stomach of the wicked shall be in want." — Proverbs 13:25 (KJV)

5. The stomach as a symbol of inner thoughts:

- "The spirit of man is the candle of the LORD, searching all the inward parts of the belly."—Proverbs 20:27 (KJV)

(Again making the connection of the brain in our head and the brain in our stomach). Imagine, God revealed in His word the connection of the two brains long before science made the discovery.

As you can see the stomach or gut is the center of our entire being for health and vitality and has a definite connection to our 'main brain.' Could it be that God is revealing just how vulnerable the gut is and how easy it is for Satan to use it to attack us? It's clear to see that throughout history, mankind has been plagued with issues concerning the gut, or the stomach. But God! Always remember the answer to all aspects of our lives is always found in God's word. God is gracious, and His provision for total health and well-being for our bodies is abundant. Let's now look to Scripture that connects the entire body to the blessings of God:

- "Trust in the LORD with all your heart, And lean not on your own understanding; In all your ways acknowledge Him, And He shall direct your paths. Do not be wise in your own eyes; Fear the LORD and depart from evil, it will be health to your flesh, And strength to your bones."— Proverbs 3:5-8 (NKJV)

It is apparent that God wants our entire body all of our DNA and all of our cells to be perfect and healthy. Remember, there are 10 times as many microbes as cells in your body and there are 100 times more DNA in your microbiome then in all the cells of your body and the DNA in both your cells and your microbiome communicate with each other. As the psalmist wrote centuries ago: "I will praise You, for I am fearfully and wonderfully made, marvelous are Your works, And that my soul knows very well."
—Psalms 139:14 (NKJV)

There are many famines throughout the world today. Many speak of a hunger soon to come upon this earth. Have we already entered a famine? There is a famine in the land, but it isn't necessarily a famine connected to food, but more so a spiritual famine. Many are suffering from a spiritual famine, and the path that millions are taking are causing them to be deceived and believe a lie. This is a fulfillment of prophecy found in 1 Timothy 4:1-2 "Now the Spirit speaketh expressly that in the latter times some shall depart from the faith, giving heed to the seducing spirits, and doctrines of devils; Speaking lies in hypocrisy; having their conscience seared with a hot iron;" (KJV). The Trinity that was from the foundation of the earth is neither antiquated nor provincial. But many believe this, and they boast that they have 'progressed' and are 'enlightened.' They say, how silly the thought of the sacred union of marriage being exclusively between 'one man and one woman.' We have control over which 'gender' we are by our 'choice' not by one that might've 'mistakenly' been given to us when we were born. There are 'many ways to heaven,' and we have evolved from the 'old rugged cross' and a 'bloody religion' to become 'gods' ourselves and guide our own destiny. The truth is they are deceived and not enlightened with their thoughts.

The Socialist Party of America has a candidate running as a Democrat. This candidate uses the word occupy. She has said on numerous occasions to occupy and proceeds to list organizations in different branches of our government to occupy. How sad to be so blind. For Jesus, Himself has told us 'occupy till I come' Luke 19:13 (KJV). They are pushing themselves further and further into spiritual darkness. Causing millions to be in a state of 'spiritual starvation.' Just as we feed our body, we must also feed our 'Spirit Man' daily. We have to get into the word of God and feed our Spirit and nurture our relationship with the true God of the universe Yahweh. It's a delicate balancing act to keep our natural body and our spiritual man in perfect health, but it's something we must do on a daily basis.

Someone just lately made a comment to me "What a saga that you have gone through." I paused, and I said, "Yeah, what a saga." I looked up the definition of saga, and it said, saga; "a long story of heroic achievement, especially medieval prose narrative in Old Norse, or Old Icelandic. A long involved story, account, or series of incidents." Well, it certainly was a long story that was involved with a series of incidents, but it didn't take place in medieval times, nor was it Icelandic. But it was in our times, these times, these days. I don't call myself heroic, but I will say 'Providence' had a hand in all of this. Providence- "the protective care of God." I will always believe with my entire being, that this miracle that I experienced was to be at this time which I believe is the end times and the power of my Heavenly Father, His Son Jesus Christ, and the Holy Spirit intervened on my behalf.

CHAPTER 21

THE EASTER MIRACLE

As I come full circle through my journey with my body being shattered, but never completely broken, I can reflect on the miracle that started that day in November and has come to fruition in March. My body may have been shattered like a piece of glass, but only by the hand of God could it be seamlessly fused together making it better than new. It was Shattered-But God!

This miracle comes at such a wonderful time of year for we are in the season of Easter. My colostomy reversal and total restoration were completed one week from the time we would celebrate that glorious Easter, or Resurrection day. But this season of Easter and Resurrection

Sunday is much different than any I've experienced before. For it has touched my life in such a way that I shall never forget.

Over 2,000 years ago my Lord Jesus Christ took the whipping and flogging repeatedly being struck by the Roman soldiers. With the full force of the leather thongs and sheep bones, they repeatedly struck and cut into His tissue ripping it open with lacerations right down to the skeletal muscles. This act caused ripples of bleeding flesh. Isaiah 53:5 (NKJV) "...And by His stripes we are healed." I am healed! These words are monumental. For what He did over 2,000 years ago applies at this moment in time for me. For me! Each whip that tore His flesh was for me in the 21st century for my complete healing and restoration. The amount of blood loss was tremendous, and His plight did not stop there. No, for it was just the beginning. He then was nailed to a cross, taunted by the soldiers, and His shed blood was for all, for the redemption of our sins. Ephesians 1:7 (NKJV) "In Him, we have redemption through His blood, the forgiveness of sins, according to the riches of His grace." The 'grace' that my Lord has given me.

The definition of the word redemption is powerful! It is the action of saving or being saved from sin, error, or evil. It is absolute. The action of regaining something in exchange for payment or clearing a debt. Our Lord cleared our debt that day. It is a free gift to those who accept it, but our Jesus paid a heavy price. Only a loving God would give His only Son, knowing it was the only way for mankind to be saved and for His Son to be the final sacrificial Lamb. To have His blood shed and do this for the whole world!

Our Heavenly Father poured out His true compassion on that day extending it into all the ages of time for every human being until that time we shall be with Him for eternity. This was done for all the world with God sacrificing His only Son. What a perfect and glorious time of year for my miracle to occur. My miracle shall never end but go on and on as a testimony of 'truth,' under 'grace,' in what my Lord Jesus Christ did for me, in this glorious season of Easter and Resurrection Sunday.

Wouldn't it be amazing if we operated as the 1st-century church seeing and experiencing the miracles of God, being Gods people that we are living now in the last days? For it indeed is the end of the age, the last of the last days. We have been given the privilege and the responsibility for living in such a time as this. We definitely can and should let God carry out miracles through us miracles that take acts of faith through the fire of the Holy Spirit. God has given all who are His "Gifts" to be stirred up and used. 2 Timothy 1:6-7 "Therefore I remind you to stir up the gift of God which is in you through the laying on of my hands. For God has not given us a spirit of fear, but of power and of love and of a sound mind." (NKJV)

We are to do and experience the supernatural power of God through the Holy Spirit. People go to church and experience 'religion' without power. Paul said those who are in Christ Jesus ought to walk even as He walked. Even the disciples wanted Jesus to increase their faith, but they didn't need their faith increased, they needed only to act on the 'faith' they had. For if they had 'faith,' they would see miracles. We have the same command today. You've been granted 'faith.' Now go and act on it. When we step out in faith believing Christ's miracle-working power, darkness will succumb to the light. Evil flees from doing good that is done in the name of Jesus, and His kingdom has overcome. Satan has but a short time, and God's word stands forever. The kingdom isn't going to come, the kingdom has come, for we are kingdom bound, and it's a done deal. All we need to do is act.

The most significant impact and influence on Christian thinking and Christianity in general sense the four Gospels are the teachings of Paul. Paul's epistles or letters to the first-century church positions us on the 'other side of the cross.' For he says, "In the time of my favor I heard you and in the day of salvation I helped you." I tell you now is the time of God's favor, now is the day of salvation." (NIV) This is where 'grace' is established for the first time in the Bible. We are now in a defined period of time known as the 'age of grace.' It's a period of time that began with the death of Christ upon the cross, also known as the 'church age.' It is a period of time defined by the teachings of Paul that we now live in today. We can see the biblical definition of grace through the following verses:

1. We are saved through Christ Jesus by grace in faith— Jude 1:3-4, Ephesians 2:8-9, James, 4:6
2. God showed us the riches of His grace through Jesus Christ — John 1:7-14, Acts 15:11, Romans 3:23-24, Titus 3:7
3. God's grace is the gift of salvation— Proverbs 3:34, Romans 5:15, Hebrews 4:16.

When you put all of these together, you can see the focus of God's 'grace' is through Christ and what he achieved on the cross for us.

It has been said, that Paul is one of the more significant New Testament authors, but the relationship of Paul of Tarsus in Judaism is still disputed today. The split of early Christianity from Judaism was gradual, and Christianity became a prominent Gentile religion. We are now in a time where we have come full circle with messianic Judaism coming to the forefront and Jews coming to the realization that Jesus or Yeshua is the Messiah.

The first century apostolic age represents a pure form of Christianity that should be adopted in the church as it exists today. Saul or Paul was hand selected by Jesus Himself. Saul was a member of the Sanhedrin and was out to destroy all remnants of Christianity. He was stopped dead in his tracks on that road to Damascus when Jesus appeared to him in a flash of light and asked him, "Saul, Saul why do you persecutest thou me?"- Acts 9:4 (KJV) From that one encounter history was never to be the same, for it was the fulfillment of God's master plan after the final atonement on the cross. The 'mystery' would only be revealed to the Apostle Paul, formally known as Saul -1 Corinthians 15:51 (NIV). We as the church are now under 'grace' and have entered a new period of time, called the 'church age.' This is the final age before Jesus returns to establish the kingdom. What a wonderfully exciting time to be alive. To be the last day's people, much like the 1st-century church here and now in the 21st century.

IN CONCLUSION

My hope and prayer after you conclude reading about my miracle, and this journey I have been on, is that the words Shattered-But God resonate in your own life. That no matter what the situation is you will get through it. Remember, the key is you go through a situation not stay in it, and God is there! God puts people in our path every day that might be experiencing a similar circumstance so we can continually encourage and help one another. Know, 'there is no respect of persons with God.' In other words, God shows no favoritism. God speaks twice on this issue in His word. "Then Peter opened his mouth and said: in truth I perceive that God shows no partiality. But in every nation whoever fears Him and works righteousness is accepted by Him" Acts 10:34- 35 (NKJV). "For there is no respect of persons with God" Romans 2:11 (KJV). If you truly believe in Him and ask with fervent prayer believing from your heart, He will hear and answer you.

If you don't know Jesus, this is the time to know Him personally. In a personal relationship. For Jesus said," I am the way, the truth, and the life no man cometh unto the Father, but by Me. All you have to do is say out loud, "Jesus is Lord and I receive You into my heart. Jesus forgive me of my sins, I believe with all of my heart You are the Son of God and died on the cross for my sins, and Your blood washes away all my past sins and makes me white as snow. I believe You rose again, and are seated at the right hand of the Father and You will come again to set up Your kingdom on the new earth that will have no end. Amen." It's that simple. You are now an eternal citizen of the Kingdom a child of our Father God Yahweh and on your way to eternal life. It's all about proclaiming the good news, the gospel. That is the great commission that Jesus commanded for all of us to do. I want to tell my story, for it is a story of a 'miracle' and of 'truth.' A story of victory by a gracious God. The true God! And I will continue to speak of it, of my miracle until God calls me home. Maranatha!

ABOUT THE AUTHOR

Lisa Pelio-Hyde, Director of Pelio School of Dance for nearly 20 years, has built a noteworthy career as a Master Ballet Teacher and Choreographer, upon the firm foundation instilled by her teacher and mother, Lena Pelio. She had the privilege during summer intensives and workshops to study with notable teachers and choreographers such as Frederick Franklin, Dennis Nahat, Stuart Sebastian, and George Zorich to name a few. As a young dancer, she was Soloist and Principal with Flint Ballet Theater. Was a featured dancer and then became director of 'Christmas at Whiting.' As well as being a soloist in Dance Detroit's annual production of 'The Nutcracker' ballet with the Detroit Symphony.

After earning her Grade VII Duo Advanced Certificate as both Dancer and Teacher in the Cecchetti Method, held by only a few in the United States at the time, she was named the first 'Young Teacher of the Year,' nationally, by the Cecchetti Council of America. She was just 23 years old and received a full scholarship to study with Margaret Marsh of London England, a former student of Maestro Cecchetti himself. She was chosen as one of 15 choreographers selected for the National Craft of Choreographers Conference in New York. She then went on to work for dance schools in Atlanta and Chicago such as the School of Atlanta Ballet, Northside High School for the Performing Arts, Ruth Mitchell Dance Company, Barat College, Chicago Dance Coalition and was a featured dancer with the Atlanta Opera.

After a decade, upon returning to Michigan, Ms. Pelio was named ballet mistress for the Michigan Opera Theatre production of 'Cinderella,' was a Governor Appointee serving two terms on the Michigan Humanities Council, and was a Michigan representative for the National Conference in Washington DC.

Lisa was nominated for the prestigious "Athena Award." She is a nationally acclaimed choreographer having her students featured in the publication for 'I Love Dance,' a well-established Dance Competition. Her students were awarded many high honors including, Overall High Score, Overall High Score in Age Category, and Cash Prizes.

Pelio School of Dance is one of the oldest established Dance Schools that has consecutively operated for nearly 80 years in Southeast Michigan. A legacy that began with Lena and continues with Lisa to this day.

Lisa was co-owner of Pelio School of Dance with her mother and became the Director during the mid-90s. She held that position till 2015 upon retiring the studio and moving with her family to the Ozarks.

REFERENCES

1. Dictionary.Cambridge.org
2. Merriam-Webster's dictionary.org
3. Wikipedia
4. Discover magazine.com
5. English standard version
6. Sepsis alliance
7. Health line -Thoracentesis
8. John Hopkins medicine.org
9. Vocabulary.com
10. metabolichealing.com
11. tacanow.org
12. Caltech
13. Rodale wellness
14. bornfitness.com

15. https://med.nyu.edu>gastro>

16. Dr. Alec.com

17. ICU steps.org

18. https://baonline.org

19. Penn med.org

20. Bible Gateway

21. Bible hub

22. www.patheos.com>blogs

23. Truth of God website

24. Curcumin the 21st century cure

25. King James Bible online.org

26. New King James Bible

27. Daily Verses.net

28. Adobe Stock images

GLOSSARY

1. Acidity

- the characteristic or state of being acid.
- sourness.

2. Alkaline

- of, containing, or similar to an alkali.
- of soil, having a pH above seven.

3. Anus

in anatomy, the opening at the lower or rear end of the intestines, through which solid waste matter is excreted.

4. Appendix

a short closed tube of tissue that projects from the pouch at the beginning of the large intestine in the lower right-hand side of the abdomen; vermiform appendix.

5. Beta Blocker

any of a class of drugs that prevent the stimulation of the adrenergic receptors responsible for increased cardiac action. Beta blockers are used to control heart rhythm, treat angina, and reduce high blood pressure.

6. Bile

a bitter yellowish secretion of the liver that aids in the digestion of fats.

7. Blood Poisoning

the presence of microorganisms or their toxins in the blood, causing disease; septicemia.

8. Borscht (borsht [or] borsch)

a hot or cold beet soup, often served with sour cream.

9. Candida

any fungus of the genus Candida that commonly causes infections, especially of the mouth and vagina.

10. Catheter

a thin, flexible, hollow tube inserted into a body passage or cavity to drain fluid, especially urine from the bladder.

11. Colitis

inflammation of the large intestine.

12. Colostomy

a surgical opening cut into the colon to allow excretion, usually made when the rectum is blocked or after surgery for colon cancer.

13. Crohn's Disease

chronic inflammatory bowel disease (IBD) characterized by inflammation of the digestive, or gastrointestinal (GI) tract.

14. CT scan

CAT scans, are special X-ray tests that produce cross-sectional images of the body using X-rays and a computer.

15. Diverticulitis

painful inflammation of a sac that branches off from a hollow organ, especially the intestine.

16. Effusion

a pouring or flowing out, or the fluid that does so.

17. Esophagus

a muscular tube from the mouth cavity to the stomach; gullet.

18. Fermentation

the chemical act or process, caused by a fermenting agent, of converting a carbohydrate into alcohol, acids, and other compounds, as yeast converts the sugar in grape juice into alcohol, producing wine.

19. Genetically Modified Foods

Genetically modified organisms (GMOs) can be defined as organisms (i.e. plants, animals or microorganisms) in which the genetic material (DNA) has been altered in a way that does not occur naturally by mating and/or natural recombination.

20. Immune System

protects the body like a guardian from harmful influences from the environment and is essential for survival.

21. Incentive Spirometer

- a device used to help you keep your lungs

healthy after surgery or when you have a lung illness, such as pneumonia.

• a device that will expand your lungs by helping you to breathe more deeply and fully.

22. Irritable Bowel Syndrome (IBS)

a common disorder that affects the large intestine. Signs and symptoms include cramping, abdominal pain, bloating, gas, and diarrhea or constipation, or both.

23. Judaism

• the monotheistic religion of the Jewish people, embodied in the Old Testament of the Bible and in the Talmud.

• the cultural, social, and spiritual identity of the Jews.

• the Jewish people.

24. Maranatha!

an Aramaic word that means "the Lord is coming" or "come, O Lord."

25. Messianic Judaism

a modern syncretic religious that combines Christianity—most importantly, the belief that Jesus is the Messiah—with elements of Judaism and Jewish tradition, its current form emerging in the 1960s and 1970s.

26. Microbe (microbes)

any microscopic life form, especially considered as a cause of infection or disease.

27. Microbiome

the microorganisms in a particular environment (including the body or a part of the body).

28. Microflora

bacteria and microscopic algae and fungi, especially those living in a particular site or habitat.

29. MRI

abbreviation of "magnetic resonance imaging," a non-invasive medical imaging technology using radio waves and powerful magnetic fields to make the interior of the human body visible in three dimensions and in real time.

30. Ornery

stubborn, mean, or disagreeable.

31. Paraphernalia

(used with a plural verb) personal possessions, especially small items.

32. Pathogen (pathogens)

any organism that causes disease, such as a bacterium or virus.

33. Perforation

the act of perforating, or the condition of being perforated.

34. Peritonitis

inflammation of the membrane that lines the abdominal cavity.

35. pH

a symbol for a measure of the degree of alkalinity or acidity of a solution, determined by the concentration or activity of hydrogen ions therein (often followed by a number, with seven indicating neutrality, zero to six indicating acidity, and eight to fourteen indicating alkalinity).

36. Physical Therapist

Physical therapists (PTs) are highly-educated, licensed health care professionals who can help patients reduce pain and improve or restore mobility - in many cases without expensive surgery and often reducing the need for long-term use of prescription medications and their side effects.

37. Pierogies

a dough dumpling stuffed with a filling such as potato or cheese, typically served with onions or sour cream.

38. Pleura (pleural)

the thin membranous sac that envelops each lung and lines the thorax in mammals.

39. Pleural Effusion

is an unusual amount of fluid around the lung.

40. Redemption

• the act of redeeming or the state of being redeemed.

• a release or rescue, as from bondage or sin.

41. Respiratory Therapist

The respiratory therapist treats people with health care issues affecting the cardiopulmonary system such as asthma, emphysema, pneumonia, cardiovascular disorders, and trauma.

42. Sanhedrin

the highest court and legislative council for secular as well as sacred matters in ancient Judea.

43. Sepsis

infection, especially by pus-forming bacteria in the blood or tissues.

44. Serotonin

an organic compound found in human and animal tissue that constricts the blood vessels and raises the blood pressure, and that is an important neurotransmitter and hormone.

45. Thoracentesis

also known as thoracocentesis or pleural tap, is an invasive procedure to remove fluid or air from the pleural space for diagnostic or therapeutic purposes.

46. Ultrasound

ultrasonic waves as used in medical diagnosis, therapy, and the like.

47. Zionism

a movement for (originally) the re-establishment and (now) the development and protection of a Jewish nation in what is now Israel. It was established as a political organization in 1897 under Theodor Herzl, and was later led by Chaim Weizmann.

APPENDIX A

1. Bishop Ron Webb

Mount Calvary Powerhouse Church
1875 Speedway Drive
Poplar Bluff, MO. 63901
(573) 686-7844
(573) 776-7335-fax
e-mail: mcpc@semo.net
http://www.ronwebbministries.com

2. Perry Stone Ministries

410 Urbane Road NE
Cleveland, TN 37312
Phone: 423-790-1717
https://www.perrystone.org

APPENDIX B

1. Lisa intubated in the Intensive Care Unit. November 17, 2017, Springfield Missouri.
2. Feelartfeelant. "Urine or pee catheter bag, - Buy This Stock Vector and Explore Similar Vectors at Adobe Stock." AdobeStock, https://stock.adobe.com/images/urine-or-pee-catheter-bag/187824508
3. Vege. "Sepsis, - Buy This Stock Vector and Explore Similar Vectors at Adobe Stock." Adobe Stock, https://stock.adobe.com/uk/images/sepsis/34280447?prev_url=detail
4. Kateryna_Kon. "Sepsis, bacteria in blood. 3D illustration showing rod-shaped bacteria in blood with red blood cells and leukocytes - - Buy This Stock Vector and Explore Similar Vectors at Adobe Stock." Adobe Stock, https://stock.adobe.com/uk/Library/d37494b7-06b8-4bf1-a5ee-2a3fd-622e9d0
5. Rob30000. "Colostomia, - Buy This Stock Vector and Explore Similar Vectors at Adobe Stock." AdobeStock, https://stock.adobe.com/images/colostomia/93029812
6. Artemida-psy . "a Colostomy Bag after Operation of Colostomy - Buy This Stock Vector and Explore Similar Vectors at Adobe Stock." Adobe Stock, https://stock.adobe.

com/images/a-colostomy-bag-afteroperation-of-colostomy/159355911?prev_url=detail.
7. Anatomy Insider. "Gut-brain connection or gut brain axis. Concept art showing a connection from the gut to the brain. 3d illustration. - Buy This Stock Vector and Explore Similar Vectors at Adobe Stock." Adobe Stock, https://stock.adobe.com/uk/Library/d37494b7-06b8-4bf1-a5ee-2a3fd-622e9d0
8. Kateryna_Kon. "Intestinal microbiome, anatomy of human digestive system andclose-up view of enteric bacteria, 3D illustration- Buy This Stock Vector andExplore Similar Vectors at Adobe Stock." Adobe Stock, https://stock.adobe.com/images/intestinal-microbiome-anatomy-of-human-digestive-system-andclose-up-view-of-enteric-bacteria-3dillustration/192214566?prev_url=detail
9. MicroOne. "Intestinal flora gut health-vector concept with bacteria and probiotics icons - Buy This Stock Vector and Explore Similar Vectors at Adobe Stock."Adobe Stock, https://stock.adobe.com/uk/images/intestinal-flora-gut-health-vectorconcept-with-bacteria-and-probioticsicons/160766053?prev_url=detail

10. Sonyakamoz. "Autumn seasonal pickled or fermented vegetables in jars placed in row over vintage kitchen drawer, white wall background, copy space. Fall home food preserving or canning - Buy This Stock Vector and Explore Similar Vectors at Adobe Stock." Adobe Stock, https://stock.adobe.com/images/autumn-seasonal-pickled-or-fermented-vegetables-injars-placed-in-row-over-vintage-kitchen-drawer-white-wall-background-copy-space-fall-home-food-preservingorcanning/175878368?prev_url=detail
11. 26. Marek. "fermented food sampler - Buy This Stock Vector and Explore Similar Vectors at Adobe Stock." Adobe Stock, https://stock.adobe.com/uk/images/fermented-food-sampler/185972436?prev_url=detail
12. Meteo021. "Jars with pickles, green tomatoes, cayenne pepper, mixed salad and chillies - Buy This Stock Vector and Explore Similar Vectors at Adobe Stock." Adobe Stock, https://stock.adobe.com/uk/Library/d37494b7-06b8-4bf1-a5ee-2a3fd-622e9d0
13. Bit24. "Organic Vegetables and legumes. -Buy This Stock Vector and Explore Similar Vectors at Adobe Stock." Adobe Stock, https://stock.adobe.com/uk/Library/d37494b7-06b8-4bf1-a5ee-2a3fd622e9d0

14. Bit24. "Fermented preserved vegetables. - Buy This Stock Vector and Explore Similar Vectors at Adobe Stock." Adobe Stock, https://stock.adobe.com/uk/Library/ d37494b7-06b8-4bf1-a5ee-2a3fd622e9d0

INDEX

A

acidity, 124–25, 151, 157–58
alkaline, 124–25, 151
ambulance, 3–5, 25
antibiotics, 6, 65
anxiety, 122–24
authority, 14–15, 42

B

bacteria, 123, 128, 156
beta blocker, 65, 87, 113–14, 151–52
blessings, 20, 67, 70–71, 75, 90, 92, 106, 133
blood pressure, 65, 87, 113–14, 160
bondage, 30, 159
bowel movement, 108
brains, 122, 132
breathing, 18, 49, 54, 56

C

cardiologist, 88, 113
catheter, 45–46, 96–97, 107, 152
Christianity, 20, 140, 142, 156
Christ Jesus, 11, 15, 57, 82, 84, 140–41

colonoscopy, 83–85, 87–88, 94
colostomy, 10–11, 65, 81, 153
commission, 18
compassion, 13, 29, 139
constipation, 155
cough, 51, 54, 103

D

darkness, 15, 62, 140
depression, 122–23
destiny, 30, 57, 99–100, 134
diseases, 26–27, 30, 122, 152, 156–57
DNA, 123, 133, 154

E

Easter, 93, 112, 137, 139
Effusion, 153
esophagus, 123, 154
evil, 56, 62, 133, 138

F

faith, 14–15, 26, 36, 67, 78–79, 88, 100, 134, 140–41
Fermentation, 128, 154
forgiveness, 138

G

gallbladder, 104
glory, 19, 92, 118–19, 130–31
GMOs (Genetically modified organisms), 128, 154
God, 18–19, 26–28, 35–39, 42–43, 55–58, 66–67, 69–71, 78–79, 83–88, 99–100, 105–7, 118–19, 129–35, 139–42, 144–45
gospel, 12–15, 18, 29–30, 61, 63, 141, 145
grace, 11, 50, 66–67, 71, 78–79, 138–39, 141–42
Gut Brain Axis, 120

H

healing, 13, 15, 27–28, 30–31, 35, 54
healing power, 18, 26
heart, 36, 43, 46, 57, 62, 75, 82, 84, 112, 133, 144–45
heart rate, 65, 87, 113–14
Holy Ghost, 28
hydrogen ions, 158

I

IBD (inflammatory bowel disease), 153
illness, 55, 118, 122, 124
Incentive Spirometer, 154
infection, 6, 11, 122–23, 152, 156, 159
inflammation, 122–23, 153, 157
inflammatory bowel disease (IBD), 153

intestine, 3, 11, 84, 114–15, 128, 151, 153
Irritable Bowel Syndrome (IBS), 122–23, 155

J

Jehovah-Rapha, 26
Jesus, 11–15, 18, 20, 29–30, 35, 42–43, 61–62, 67, 95, 135, 139–40, 142, 145, 156
Judaism, 60, 142, 155–56

K

kingdom, 15, 30, 56, 61, 63, 140, 142, 145

L

lacerations, 138
light, 30, 41, 62–63, 87, 93, 140, 142
love, 66–67, 72, 75, 80, 90, 107, 140
loyalty, 62

M

Maranatha, 82, 145, 155
medications, 68, 87, 124, 130
microbes, 123, 133, 156
microbiome, 123, 133, 156
microflora, 128, 156
microorganisms, 128, 152, 154, 156
mind, 21–22, 24, 26, 31, 33, 61–62, 66–67, 78, 84–86, 106, 113, 116, 131

miracles, 6, 11–15, 75, 112–13, 118–19, 135, 137, 139–40, 144–45
MRI, 54–55, 156

N

neurotransmitter, 160

O

outpouring, 40, 61–62
oxygen, 51, 54
oxygen level, 113

P

pain, 4, 158
pain pump, 95, 102
pathogens, 124–25, 157
peace, 5, 29, 48, 56, 58, 84
Perforation, 157
perseverance, 19, 107
pleural space, 54, 160
pleural tap, 160
pneumonia, 51, 155, 159
power, 16, 28, 31, 35, 66–67, 91, 136, 140
prayer, 16, 19, 26–27, 33, 47, 78, 84–85, 88, 90–92, 95, 107, 129, 144

President Trump, 58, 60
prophecy, 59, 134

PT (Physical therapists), 32–34, 49–50, 69–70, 158

R

redemption, 20, 138, 159
respiratory therapist, 51, 159
restoration, 138
reversal, 83, 88, 115–16
reversal surgery, 65, 89
Revelation 12, 60
righteousness, 27, 35, 144

S

salvation, 36, 141
Satan, 30, 66, 84, 132, 140
seasons, 60, 137
sepsis, 6, 8, 11, 159
servant, 14–15
sickness, 26, 30
skeletal muscles, 138
staff, 19, 24, 41–42
steadfastness, 61
stoma, 10–11, 76–77, 88, 91, 102
stomach, 34, 86, 103–5, 110, 113, 122, 124, 131–32, 154
stoma site, 46, 94–95, 115
strength, 32, 34–36, 70, 80–81, 133

surgeon, 6, 11, 34, 38–39, 52–55, 65, 68, 83–84, 88, 90, 96, 101–5, 109, 112, 114–15
surgery, 6, 11, 55–56, 87, 89–92, 95, 101, 103–5, 107–8, 111–12, 153, 155
surgical soap, 94
survival, 8, 154

T

teacher, 146
testimony, 12, 18, 139
Thoracentesis, 54, 149, 160
tissues, 115, 151, 159
tribulations, 85

U

Ultrasound, 160

W

weaknesses, 66–67
worldliness, 131

Y

Yahweh, 119

Z

Zionism, 59, 160

www.ingramcontent.com/pod-product-compliance
Lightning Source LLC
Chambersburg PA
CBHW052132110526
44591CB00012B/1694